Very Good Salads.

SHUKI & LOUISA

Very Good Salads.

Middle Eastern salads & plates for sharing

Smith
Street
Books

FEL

with 3 falafel balls / without

$15 / $12

ash $13 / $10

hus $7

SALADS

~WHITE BEAN, ARTICHOKE,
~ONFI

contents

introduction

Very Good Falafel is a little falafel shop on Brunswick's busy Sydney Road in Melbourne, Australia. It's small, less than 20 seats, and is open for lunch and dinner six days a week. The menu is based on Shuki's mum's Iraqi Jewish upbringing, and centres around super-green, very fresh falafel made with lots of herbs and spices. In addition to falafel, we make our own version of the Iraqi Jewish street-food sandwich, sabih, filled with fried eggplant, potato, chopped tomato and cucumber, pickles, zhough, amba and lots of tahini sauce, all stuffed into a fluffy pita pocket. Our only meat dish is ktzitzot, which are lamb meatballs made with lots of parsley and spices. These dishes are on our menu every day. What changes are the four salads we make, usually with roasted vegetables, grains, herbs, nuts and pulses, with lots of olive oil, lemon juice and tahini. The idea behind these rotating seasonal dishes, alongside our menu staples, is to create something new so our customers will never get bored! So, every day, except Sundays, since 2016, we have written a new salad menu every morning, based on what looks good at the local market and what we feel like eating.

The story of our friendship and little falafel shop began, and continues, in Brunswick. We met in a big share house on Blyth Street, and after living together and cooking together we eventually had the idea to sell dips at farmers' markets. We started small – very, very small – with a borrowed car, some eskies, a commercial kitchen that belonged to the Cultivating Community in Fitzroy, a farmers' market marquee and not much else! During the week we'd make dips – hummus, baba ghanoush, harissa and muhammara – and sell them on Saturdays and Sundays at the markets around Melbourne. After a few years, we decided to start selling falafel as well. The response was overwhelming, but especially so at our Wednesday lunchtime slot at Melbourne University. Our market team grew from one person to seven, and suddenly people wanted to know where they could buy our falafel every day. We started looking for spaces to rent on Sydney Road in early 2016, and found the former Italian bakery where we still work today.

It would be hard to imagine a better partnership for a falafel business than the daughter of a chickpea farmer and the son of an Iraqi Jewish cooking legend, but it's true! Louisa was born in Wycheproof in north-western Victoria. Both sides of her family have been farming grains and pulses for years, and the smell of barley and chickpeas in big bags at the back of our shop is a constant reminder of Louisa's time growing up in the country, and the dusty Christmas-time grain harvests. Shuki was born in Netanya, Israel, to a Romanian dad and Iraqi mum, whose ancestors had lived in Iraq for thousands of years before events led them to Israel in the 1950s. Shuki's mother taught him how to prepare traditional family dishes, although when we met Shuki was cooking steak and chips at French restaurants and pubs, and Louisa was a primary-school art teacher. Cooking together and starting a business gave us both a way to connect with something that was true to us, as well as doing something we enjoyed!

Our goal from the beginning, with the dips, with Very Good Falafel, was always to make good-quality Middle-Eastern food that we could be proud of and that was accessible to everyone. At Very Good Falafel we keep our prices low and the quality high. The goal with this book is the same: we want people to eat delicious food every day. The ingredients for most of the recipes can be found at your local supermarket, although a few require some special in-season ingredients, which might mean a conversation with your greengrocer or a walk around your neighbourhood. Most of the salads work well as side dishes or grouped together as part of a spread. Simply choose two or three salads from the same season, whip up some tahini sauce, pita and, of course, some falafel, and you're ready for a feast!

the very good salads pantry

AMBA

Although the name of our shop is Very Good Falafel, in reality we would be nothing without amba, an Iraqi mango turmeric pickle that's made with fermented mango, mustard, turmeric and fenugreek. It goes beautifully with hummus and zhough. You will find our recipe on page 180.

DATE MOLASSES

There is no sugar in our kitchen, so we normally use fresh and dried fruits and berries to sweeten things up. But there is nothing really as sweet as dates … they're just pure balls of caramel. Date molasses is so sweet, we mostly like to pair it with slightly bitter nuts and seeds such as walnuts and sesame seeds. Look for bottles of molasses that contain only dates and no sugar; Iraqi ones are the best.

DRIED LEGUMES AND PULSES

It's not too dramatic to say that pulses are our life! We always prefer dried over tinned: add plenty of onions, bay leaves and olive oil to the cooking water and you'll have a lovely tasting 'stock' when you're done. Also, for making salads, there's nothing quite like freshly cooked beans, chickpeas (garbanzo beans) and lentils, dressed in really good olive oil and lemon juice.

FRESH ZA'ATAR

Za'atar is the Eastern child of the oregano family. Its leaves are furry and it tastes less punchy and more delicate than its Italian and Greek siblings. While the za'atar spice mix most of us know is usually, though not limited to, a combination of salt, oregano, sumac and sesame,

we often prefer fresh and solo when we can find it. The best way to get your hands on this herb is to visit a nursery (its boring name is *Origanum Syriacum*) and buy a little plant for your veggie patch or windowsill.

GREEN ALMONDS

Unripened almonds are available from some fruit and vegetable grocers and farmers' markets during spring. If you can't find any, then check your local neighbourhood for almond trees and pick your own! We love to slice them up very thinly and toss them with crunchy things like raw fennel and kohlrabi.

HARISSA

There are a lot of magical condiments out there, but harissa might be the most magical of all! Originating from Tunisia, it's found all over the world now and is popular in Israel with the North African diaspora. We make it often at the shop with soaked dried chillies, lemon, garlic and spices. It's incredible with potatoes, pumpkin and spread on a baguette. You will find our recipe on page 176.

NUTS

In our recipes we recommend freshly roasting nuts in a low oven. We always try to buy them raw and finish the cooking ourselves on the day they are served.

PILPELCHUMA

This mix of paprikas, crushed garlic and olive oil is the foundation for the perfect matbucha, shakshuka or just as a spread on bread or veggies. You will find our recipe on page 187.

POMEGRANATE MOLASSES

We really wish we could get pomegranates all year round! But it's impossible, well sort of ... we buy all the pomegranates we can while they are in season, juice them and reduce the liquid over low heat, then store it in jars to use in salad dressings, dishes with grains and the occasional cheeky teaspoon straight into our mouths!

PRESERVED LEMON

There is something in the flavour of preserved lemons that is like nothing else; umami is an understatement, and the result of this sour fruit mixed with salt is almost sweet. Magic. We normally use the skin in salads, sliced into strips, and the juicy bit we turn into a paste in the food processor. See pages 179 and 151 for recipes.

TAHINI SAUCE

There is nothing to say here other than tahini goes with everything! This is how we make our tahini sauce:

135 g (½ cup) tahini
2 tablespoons lemon juice
big pinch of sea salt flakes

Place the tahini in the bowl of a food processor. Add the lemon juice and salt, then with the motor running, slowly drizzle in 250 ml (1 cup) of water. It will thicken up quickly, but keep adding the water until the mixture is the texture of thickened cream You can also do this in a bowl with a wooden spoon or fork.

TORSHI

Shuki grew up eating these crunchy, juicy Iraqi pickles. Torshi is a great way to lighten a heavy meal, or to aid digestion when eating fried food. You will find our recipe on page 184.

ZHOUGH

This is a Yemenite chilli sauce made with green chillies, coriander (cilantro), garlic and lots of spices. Our recipe comes from Shuki's friend's dad, Moti, who is from Sana'a in Yemen. We make it just as he did, and in big batches because everything tastes boring without zhough! Check out page 187 for our recipe.

spring

bulgur wheat, saffron, broad bean and dill pilaf —— stuffed mulberry leaves —— celery, radish, mint, broad beans, spring onion —— green plum, celery, French lentils —— confit rainbow silverbeet —— ruby grapefruit, green almonds, wild fennel —— broad bean and macadamia-stuffed artichokes —— artichokes, broad beans, radish, fried pita —— leek papillote —— charoset in cos leaf —— asparagus, capers, green almonds, preserved lemon

bulgur wheat, saffron, broad bean and dill pilaf

Coarse bulgur wheat is one of our favourite grains to use at the shop, and this dish is one of our most popular ways to use it! Inspired by Persian pilafs with dill and broad beans, this is a real springtime treat.

SERVES 4

100 g (3½ oz) shelled pistachios
500 g (1 lb 2 oz) broad (fava) beans
1 tablespoon extra virgin olive oil
1 brown onion, sliced
big pinch of saffron threads
sea salt flakes and freshly ground black pepper
200 g (1 cup) coarse bulgur wheat
2 bay leaves (preferably fresh)
1 cinnamon stick
60 g (⅓ cup) fresh or frozen peas
2 tablespoons chopped parsley
2 tablespoons chopped mint leaves
2 tablespoons dill fronds

Preheat the oven to 160°C (320°F) fan-forced. Spread the pistachios over a baking tray and bake for 8–10 minutes, until fragrant. Be careful not to overcook. Cool and chop the pistachios.

Pod the broad beans, then peel them again. This is easier if you give them a quick soak in hot water first.

Heat the olive oil in a large heavy-based frying pan over medium heat. Add the onion and cook for 10 minutes or until soft. Add the saffron threads and a big pinch of salt, give the mixture a stir and add the bulgur wheat. Pour enough water into the pan to cover the mixture by 5 cm (2 in), then add the bay leaves and cinnamon stick. Bring to the boil, then reduce the heat to a simmer, cover and cook for 15 minutes or until soft, checking halfway through to make sure the bulgur isn't drying out – add a little more water if necessary. Add the broad beans and peas in the last 5 minutes of cooking.

Remove the pan from the heat and check you're happy with the seasoning. Add the herbs just before serving and scatter over the pistachios to finish.

Serve warm.

stuffed mulberry leaves

In early spring, when vine leaves are still too small to use, the mulberry tree is there for you.

In fact, unlike grape leaves that hide a bit of sourness, mulberry leaves are quite sweet. Make sure to pick them while they are soft and fresh, before any fruit has ripened on the tree. Try to find the biggest leaves you can, to make your life easier later on.

MAKES 40

300 g (1½ cups) basmati or jasmine rice
50 g (⅓ cup) toasted pine nuts
40 large mulberry leaves
125 ml (½ cup) extra virgin olive oil
1 brown onion, diced
½ bunch of mint, leaves chopped
½ bunch of dill, fronds chopped
2 lemons: 1 zested, 1 sliced
sea salt flakes and freshly ground black pepper
2 tomatoes, cut into 1 cm (½ in) thick slices
60 ml (¼ cup) pomegranate molasses

Put the rice in a bowl, cover generously with water and set aside to soak for 1 hour. Drain.

Heat a frying pan over medium heat, add the pine nuts and toast, stirring frequently, for 2–3 minutes, until golden and fragrant.

Bring a large saucepan of water to the boil over high heat and blanch the mulberry leaves in batches for 30 seconds. Drain the mulberry leaves and refresh under cold water, then transfer to a clean dry tea towel to dry out.

Heat 2 tablespoons of the olive oil in a frying pan over medium heat. Add the onion and sauté for 10 minutes or until a light golden colour. Remove from the heat and stir in the rice, herbs, lemon zest and pine nuts and season with salt and pepper.

Drizzle 2 tablespoons of the remaining oil over the base of a large heavy-based saucepan, then cover the base with the tomato slices and season with salt and pepper.

On a comfortable working space, place a mulberry leaf with its wide end closest to you. Place a tablespoon of the rice mixture in the centre of the leaf, then fold in the sides and roll up to enclose the mixture firmly. Call someone to give you a hand because you have 39 more to go.

Tightly pack the stuffed leaves on top of the tomato in the saucepan, starting from the edge and working inwards, creating an inner circle as well. If you need to stack a second layer, go for it. Top with the lemon slices and pour over the pomegranate molasses and remaining oil. Add enough water to come to the top of the stuffed leaves and place an upside-down plate on top to keep the leaves in place. Cover with a lid and bring to the boil over medium–high heat, then reduce the heat to low and cook, covered, for 1–1½ hours, until the rice is tender. Serve warm or at room temperature.

Any leftovers will keep in an airtight container in the fridge for 1–2 days, covered with a layer of olive oil.

celery, radish, mint, broad beans, spring onion

This is what we want to eat every day in spring! Fresh, crunchy and colourful, with the broad beans reminding us of their short but sweet season.

SERVES 4

400 g (14 oz) broad (fava) beans
½ bunch of celery, cut into 5 mm (¼ in) thick slices
    on the diagonal
5–6 radishes, cut into thin wedges
2 handfuls of mint leaves
4 spring onions (scallions), thinly sliced
100 ml (3½ fl oz) extra virgin olive oil
juice of 1 lemon
sea salt flakes

Pod the broad beans, then peel them again. This is easier if you give them a quick soak in hot water first.

Place the double-podded beans, celery, radish, mint leaves and spring onion in a bowl. Drizzle over the olive oil and lemon juice, scatter with sea salt and toss gently to combine.

Serve immediately.

green plum, celery, French lentils

There are two groups of spring produce. First are the vegetables that grow only in springtime and must be eaten at their peak – artichokes, broad beans, asparagus, crunchy carrots, endless varieties of radish ... The second group is produce that won't be ready until summer but we can't bear to wait that long, so we pick them early and find ways to use them! This is the case when it comes to green almonds, which we harvest as soon as our eyes spot fruit on the tree. We slice them thinly and basically eat the shell with the almond inside in jelly form. The same is true for freekeh, which is basically wheat that didn't get a chance to dry in the sun and is instead harvested fresh and placed over fire to make it possible to separate the grain from the pod. The result is a grain that tastes light with a hint of smoky flavour. Then there's garlic that's often pulled from the ground before it gets a chance to divide into cloves; the young bulbs soft and aromatic.

This recipe doesn't contain any of these ingredients – we are her for the plums. Of course ripe plums have their place on the kitchen table, but green plums should be up there too, with their lovely sourness that balances the earthiness of lentils and neutral flavour of celery in this salad.

When we pick green plums from my own tree, I normally take the ones at the top that the birds are eyeing up, or any with funny marks. If you don't happen to have a plum tree, you can find green plums at farmers' markets and Turkish and Middle Eastern grocers.

SERVES 6

500 g (2½ cups) French (puy) lentils
300 g (10½ oz) green plums, stoned and diced
6 celery stalks, diced
1 red onion, diced
125 ml (½ cup) extra virgin olive oil
juice of 2 lemons
sea salt flakes

Bring a large saucepan of water to the boil over high heat. Add the lentils, then reduce the heat to a simmer and cook for about 20 minutes or until the lentils are just tender. Drain and allow to cool to room temperature.

Place the lentils, plum, celery and onion in a bowl. Drizzle over the olive oil and lemon juice and season with salt, to taste. Toss well to combine and serve straight away.

Any leftovers will keep in an airtight container in the fridge for 2–3 days.

confit rainbow silverbeet

Marcello, our farmer, is famous for his artichokes and cauliflowers of which he grows the best in Melbourne. But with every delivery he also includes a couple of big boxes packed with the freshest, most colourful bunches of rainbow silverbeet you've seen. We cook them in every possible way, from pickling or frying the stalks to stuffing the leaves, making stews and fresh salads. In this dish, we confit the stalks, which makes them melt in your mouth like butter. We garnish the stalks with a few peas and kale flowers, simply because we love them so much.

SERVES 4

bunch of rainbow silverbeet (Swiss chard) stalks, trimmed
 (save the leaves to make the stuffed silverbeet leaves
 on page 117)
3 slices of lemon
1 bay leaf (preferably fresh)
1 garlic clove, peeled
1 dried long red chilli
2 tablespoons coriander seeds
olive oil, to confit
handful of fresh peas
kale flowers or mustard flowers, to serve (optional)

TIP

Strain the leftover oil into a jar, discarding the leftover solids in the pan. The lightly flavoured oil can be reused as it hasn't boiled.

Lay the silverbeet stalks flat in a large frying pan or saucepan and add the lemon, bay leaf, garlic, chilli and a pinch of the coriander seeds. Add enough olive oil to cover the stalks.

Place the pan over the lowest possible heat and confit, uncovered, for about 50 minutes, until the silverbeet stalks are very soft. Don't let the oil come to a simmer.

Meanwhile, heat a frying pan over medium heat and toast the remaining coriander seeds for 5 minutes or until fragrant.

Bring a small saucepan of water to the boil and blanch the peas for 2–3 minutes. Drain and rinse under cold water to stop the cooking process.

Remove the silverbeet stalks from the pan using a slotted spoon, then transfer to a serving dish. Scatter the peas, flowers (if using) and toasted coriander seeds over the top and serve at room temperature

ruby grapefruit, green almonds, wild fennel

This dish screams freshness – it's all you want when the sun is starting to find its way out from behind the clouds ... especially with a glass of arak on the side.

SERVES 2

3 ruby grapefruit, segmented
5 green almonds, thinly sliced
1–2 wild fennel stalks (you can also use regular sliced fennel stalks)
½ long green chilli, deseeded and thinly sliced
sea salt flakes and freshly ground black pepper
2 tablespoons extra virgin olive oil

Toss the grapefruit, almond and fennel together in a large bowl.

Transfer the salad to a serving bowl, scatter the chilli over the top and season to taste with salt and pepper. Drizzle the olive oil over the top and serve.

Cheers!

broad bean and macadamia-stuffed artichokes

With all respect to the person who invented the wheel, we are more grateful to the person who figured out that artichokes are edible. Who would have thought to pick this big flower while it's still closed, boil it, discard about 70 per cent of it, including most of the leaves and the furry flower buds, and then bite into the flower base while holding it like it's the holy grail ...

In this recipe we stuff the holy grail with the best of the best, aka broad beans and macadamia nuts. Wherever you are the person who discovered the artichoke – thank you!

MAKE 6

2 lemons
2 bay leaves (preferably fresh)
sea salt flakes and freshly ground black pepper
6 artichokes
100 g (3½ oz) macadamia nuts
500 g (1 lb 2 oz) broad (fava) beans, podded
10 mint leaves, chopped
10 parsley leaves, chopped

Preheat the oven to 160°C (320°F) fan-forced.

Fill a large wide saucepan with 5 cm (2 in) of water, squeeze in the juice from 1 lemon and throw in the bay leaves and 2 teaspoons of salt.

Working with one artichoke at a time, remove the tough outer leaves and trim the stalk. Slice off the top half of the artichoke and, using a small spoon, scoop out and discard the fluffy choke.

Place the cleaned, hollowed-out artichokes upside down in the prepared pan. Bring to the boil over medium–high heat, then reduce the heat to a simmer, cover and cook for 20–25 minutes, until the artichokes can be easily pierced with a toothpick.

Meanwhile, spread the macadamias over a baking tray and bake for about 10 minutes, until fragrant and lightly coloured. Set aside to cool.

Bring a saucepan of water to the boil over high heat and blanch the broad beans for 2 minutes. Drain and refresh in cold water and then pod them again.

Using a sharp knife or a food processor, separately dice or pulse the macadamias and broad beans until finely chopped. You want them small but still retaining some bite, without being mushy.

Combine the macadamias, broad beans, mint, parsley and juice from the remaining lemon in a bowl and season to taste with salt and pepper. Using a spoon, evenly stuff the hollowed-out artichokes with the broad bean mixture, then serve.

artichokes, broad beans, radish, fried pita

Punchy with so many of spring's best things – artichokes, broad beans and broad bean leaves – this salad is a real celebration of the season!

SERVES 4

400 g (14 oz) broad (fava) beans
2 lemons
3 artichokes
125 ml (½ cup) extra virgin olive oil
1 Greek-style pita bread
sea salt flakes
3 handfuls of tender young broad beans leaves, picked
   (you can also use baby spinach)
5–6 radishes, thinly sliced
handful of mint leaves
Tahini sauce (see page 11), to serve

Pod the broad beans, then peel them again. This is easier if you give them a quick soak in hot water first.

Fill a large non-reactive bowl with water and squeeze in the juice from one of the lemons.

Working with one artichoke at a time, remove the tough outer leaves and trim the stalk. Slice off the top half of the artichoke and, using a small spoon, scoop out and discard the fluffy choke. Cut the artichokes into medium wedges through the stalk and place in the prepared bowl.

Heat 2 tablespoons of the olive oil in a large frying pan over high heat. Tear the pita into bite-sized pieces and brown for 2–3 minutes each side, taking care not to burn the pieces. Place on paper towel to drain and season with salt.

Remove the artichoke from the water and drain well. Toss with 2 tablespoons of the remaining oil, then place in a frying pan over medium heat and fry for 2–3 minutes each side, until lightly golden and slightly crisp.

Combine the broad beans, artichoke, broad bean leaves, radish and mint leaves in a bowl, then drizzle with the juice from the remaining lemon, along with the remaining oil. Toss very gently to combine.

Serve with tahini on the side.

leek papillote

If the days of the week were onions, Monday to Friday would probably be the brown onion, and the weekend would be the leek. With its head showing off up high rather than being buried under the soil, the leek seems confident enough to handle it all by itself.

Here, we use the French papillote technique to cook the leek, then finish it with harissa, because everything is better with a bit of harissa, and the leek knows it couldn't ask for a better wingman.

SERVES 4

4 leeks, white and pale green parts, washed well
sea salt flakes
extra virgin olive oil, for drizzling
2 tablespoons Harissa (see page 176)
chopped chives, to serve

Preheat the oven to 160°C (320°F) fan-forced. Cut four large sheets of baking paper about 40 cm (16 in) long.

Place one leek in each sheet of baking paper, then sprinkle generously with salt and drizzle over a good glug of olive oil. Enclose the leeks by rolling up and tightening the ends of the baking paper. Transfer to a large baking dish and bake the leeks for 1 hour or until soft.

Cut a long slit through the baking paper and the leek, add 2 teaspoons of harissa to each parcel, along with a few chopped chives. Serve hot and enjoy your weekend.

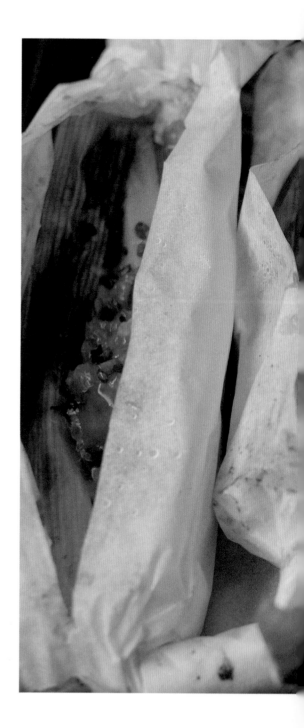

charoset in cos leaf

Every year around March/April it's Pesach (Passover) time. First, this means a lot of cleaning, and I mean a lot of cleaning. The kind of cleaning when you really need your bond money back asap and you know you are dealing with a dodgy landlord. The reason is to eliminate even the tiniest breadcrumb in the house during the week of the holiday when bread is forbidden ... kind of a celiac festival, I guess.

Secondly, it means a lot of cooking! When I was growing up, the food on our Pesach table changed every year and didn't have a special theme, but before you got to the food there was a long night of reading, singing and blessing ahead. The blessing is done over a plate with plain ingredients, such as egg, bitter herbs, lamb shank, matza and horseradish, each one representing something specific and eaten one at a time. But then comes the charoset which gives a whole new spin to the plate.

It is meant to look like clay, to represent the hard work undertaken by slaves in ancient Egypt. It is different in every Jewish culture, depending on your location – Ashkenazi Jews use a mixture of apples, walnuts and red wine, while us Iraqi Jews lucked out with the sweetest version of all – containing date molasses and walnuts – served on crunchy cos lettuce leaves.

MAKES 12

2 baby cos (romaine) lettuce
150 ml (5 fl oz) premium date molasses (not syrup)
200 g (7 oz) walnuts
finely grated zest of 1 lemon
5 mint leaves, shredded
extra virgin olive oil, for drizzling

Find the crunchiest cos leaves you can and wash them well. You'll need 12 leaves for this recipe.

Mix the molasses and walnuts together in a bowl to make the charoset.

Place a spoonful of charoset on top of each leaf and garnish with lemon zest and mint. Drizzle with olive oil and serve.

asparagus, capers, green almonds, preserved lemon

Tart green almonds and grilled asparagus are a beautiful-looking (and tasty!) combination. Make this salad using the green almonds you've picked from your neighbours' almond tree.

SERVES 4

350–400 g (12½–14 oz) asparagus, woody ends trimmed
1 tablespoon extra virgin olive oil, plus extra for drizzling
sea salt flakes and freshly ground black pepper
100 g (3½ oz) green almonds, thinly sliced
1 tablespoon salted capers, rinsed
2 pieces of Preserved Lemon (see page 179), skin only,
   thinly sliced

Bring a large saucepan of salted water to the boil and blanch the asparagus for 1–2 minutes, until bright green. Drain and refresh in cold water, then pat dry. Set aside.

Heat the olive oil in a chargrill pan or frying pan with the over medium–high heat. Cook the asparagus until lightly charred, then transfer to a serving platter, season with salt and pepper and drizzle with a little extra olive oil. Top with the almonds, capers and preserved lemon and serve warm.

summer

Romanian eggplant (salata de vinete) —— cucumber, dates, pistachio —— bulgur-stuffed tomatoes, saffron, mint —— zucchini, harissa, black olives, mint —— watermelon fattoush —— tomato, capsicum, eggplant bake —— mashwiya salad —— roasted eggplant, mango, amba, green chilli —— peaches, basil, hazelnuts —— frozen grapes, herbs, zucchini flowers —— cherries, walnuts, coriander, green chilli —— grilled apricot, warrigal greens, saffron oil, hazelnuts —— harissa —— chickpeas, fava, fresh tomato sauce —— red pepper involtini —— tomatoes in pomegranate sauce

Romanian eggplant (salata de vinete)

There are two things that make me especially proud of my dad's Romanian side of the family.

The first is the appearance of the Romanian football team at the 1994 World Cup where Gheorghe Haji and Ilie Dumitrescu took the team all the way to the quarter final, including a 3:2 win over Argentina, before losing to Sweden by penalty shootout. Haji was an absolute superstar and known as the Maradona of the Carpathians; Dumitrescu, on the other hand, had much less glam on his boot but was always there to push the ball over the line.

The second thing is this eggplant dish. This five-ingredient super-simple recipe is the missing link for the perfect mezze and the best companion to whatever protein comes out of the barbecue.

The eggplant is the star – just like Haji – but it's the unapologetic raw diced onion and crushed garlic that pushes the ball over the line ...

Cook the eggplants over an open flame for 10–15 minutes, turning with tongs every 5 minutes, until the skin is burnt all over and the flesh is soft. Remove from the heat and place in a bowl until it is cool enough to handle.

Peel the eggplants and place the flesh in a colander for any liquid to drain. Discard the skin and stalks (the skin is excellent for the compost).

Transfer the eggplant to a bowl and smash using a fork until smooth, then add the onion, garlic, salt, pepper and olive oil. Stir well to combine.

Place the eggplant mixture in a serving dish, scatter over the mint and Aleppo pepper, drizzle with a little extra oil and serve at room temperature.

SERVES 6

4 eggplants (aubergines)
1 brown onion, diced
3 garlic cloves, crushed
1 teaspoon sea salt flakes
½ teaspoon freshly ground black pepper
60 ml (¼ cup) extra virgin olive oil, plus extra for drizzling
5 mint leaves, chopped
Aleppo pepper, for sprinkling

cucumber, dates, pistachio

The combination of how easy this salad is to make and how tasty it is, drives us to put it on the table. It's just how we like it when it's hot. An easy and yummy salad that no one's gonna say no to!

SERVES 4

70 g (½ cup) shelled pistachios
3 Lebanese cucumbers
6 Medjool dates, pitted, each date sliced into 6 strips
½ red onion, diced
handful of chives, chopped
finely grated zest of ½ lemon, plus a little juice
sea salt flakes
extra virgin olive oil, for drizzling

Preheat the oven to 160°C (320°F) fan-forced. Spread the pistachios over a baking tray and bake for 8–10 minutes, until fragrant. Take care not to overcook. Cool and chop the pistachios.

Cut the cucumbers in half lengthways and scrape out the seeds with a teaspoon. Cut into 5 mm (¼ in) thick half moons. Combine the cucumber, date, onion, chives, lemon zest and pistachios in a bowl. Dress with a little squeeze of lemon juice, a pinch of salt and a drizzle of olive oil, and serve.

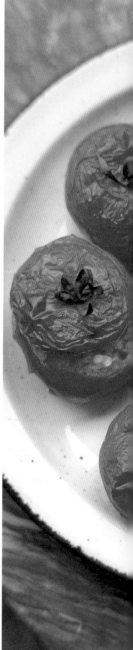

bulgur-stuffed tomatoes, saffron, mint

The method for cooking these tomatoes comes from a couple of very inspiring cooks, Rachel Roddy and Carla Tomasi. We change up the filling a bit, but the idea is similar: tomatoes so juicy and ripe that they taste just like tomato sauce, and a garlicky filling that reminds us of why we love stuffing things so much!

SERVES 8

8 large vine-ripened tomatoes with stems
sea salt flakes and freshly ground black pepper
100 g (½ cup) coarse bulgur wheat
2 tablespoons chopped mint leaves
2 garlic cloves, finely chopped or grated
big pinch of saffron threads
2 tablespoons extra virgin olive oil

Remove the top 1 cm (½ in) from the tomatoes and set aside. Scoop out the tomato flesh and place it in a bowl. Sprinkle a pinch of salt inside each hollowed-out tomato, then turn upside-down on a clean tea towel and leave to drain.

Blend the tomato flesh with a stick blender or food processor and season well with salt and pepper. Add the bulgur wheat, mint, garlic and saffron. Stir well and allow to sit for 45 minutes.

Preheat the oven to 160°C (320°F) fan-forced. Lightly grease a roasting tin, that will snugly fit the tomatoes, with olive oil.

Fill each tomato three-quarters full with the bulgur mixture and place the 'lids' back on. Place the stuffed tomatoes in the prepared tin and bake for about 1 hour, until they are slightly shrivelled and the bulgur is cooked. Remove from the oven and allow to sit for 30 minutes before serving.

zucchini, harissa, black olives, mint

The idea of steamed zucchini probably doesn't sound that exciting, but the magic of harissa prevails once again here! It's such a magical spice, taking any and every vegetable to great heights, even steamed zucchini.

SERVES 4

3 zucchini (courgettes), cut into 1.5 cm (½ in) pieces
sea salt flakes and freshly ground black pepper
2 tablespoons chopped parsley
2 tablespoons chopped mint leaves
handful of pitted kalamata olives, halved

HARISSA DRESSING

2 tablespoons Harissa (see page 176)
2 tablespoons extra virgin olive oil
juice of 1 lemon

Steam the zucchini over a saucepan of boiling water for 5–10 minutes, until very soft.

Meanwhile, whisk the dressing ingredients together in a small bowl. While still warm, dress the zucchini, mixing very well so the zucchini is completely coated. Taste for seasoning and set aside for 10 minutes. When the zucchini has cooled a little, add the herbs and olives, then serve straight away.

watermelon fattoush

To be honest, we feel a bit guilty for replacing the tomato in this fattoush with watermelon, but the outcome is worth the guilt. This is still good-old fattoush salad, just with a twist to get you through the hottest days of summer.

SERVES 4

1 Lebanese cucumber
120 ml (4 fl oz) extra virgin olive oil
1 Greek-style pita bread, torn into bite-sized pieces
sea salt flakes
1 teaspoon smoked paprika
⅛ watermelon, peeled and cut into 2 cm (¾ in) cubes
6 radishes, quartered
½ bunch of mint, leaves torn
¼ red onion, thinly sliced
juice of 1 lemon
½ teaspoon ground sumac

Cut the cucumber in half lengthways and slice into half moons, about 1 cm (½ in) thick.

Heat 2 tablespoons of the olive oil in a frying pan over medium–high heat. Add the pita pieces and cook, stirring, for 2–3 minutes each side, until golden and crunchy all over. Using a slotted spoon, transfer the pita croutons to a large bowl and season with salt and the paprika. Set aside to cool to room temperature.

Add the cucumber, watermelon, radish, mint and onion to the bowl with the pita croutons. Drizzle with the lemon juice and remaining olive oil, and season with a little more salt if necessary. Place in a serving dish, sprinkle with the sumac and serve.

tomato, capsicum, eggplant bake

The holy trinity of summer vegetables, putting on a show together ...

SERVES 6

2 red capsicums (bell peppers)
2 eggplants (aubergines)
4 tomatoes
sea salt flakes and freshly ground black pepper
extra virgin olive oil, for drizzling
oregano leaves, to serve

Preheat the oven to 200°C (400°F) fan-forced.

Place the capsicums on a baking tray and roast for about 35 minutes, until the skins are black and starting to separate from the flesh. Set aside in a bowl, covered, for 10 minutes, then peel and cut into 4–5 cm (1½–2 in) wide strips. Reduce the oven temperature to 150°C (300°F) fan-forced.

Cook the eggplant over an open flame for 10–15 minutes, turning with tongs every 5 minutes, until the skin is burnt all over and the flesh is soft. Remove from the heat and place in a bowl until cool enough to handle, then peel and slice into 4–5 cm (1½–2 in) wide strips.

Next, score a shallow cross in the base of each tomato. Bring a saucepan of water to the boil, add the tomatoes and blanch for 2 minutes or until the skin starts to come away from the base of each tomato. Using a slotted spoon, scoop the tomatoes into a bowl of cold water and leave to cool. Peel the tomatoes, then cut in half and cut again into 2 cm (¾ in) thick slices.

Place the vegetables on a work surface and season well with salt and pepper, then layer the capsicum, tomato and eggplant in a 20 × 10 cm (8 × 4 in) baking dish. Drizzle generously with olive oil, then transfer to the oven and bake for 1 hour. Increase the temperature to 180°C (350°F) fan-forced for a final 10–15 minutes, until the tops of the vegetables are crisp.

Sprinkle with oregano leaves and serve warm.

mashwiya salad

Mashwi means grill, and if you love your barbecue do it a favour and cook this salad on it.

Hailing from Tunisia, this dish pays homage to tomatoes and capsicums by cooking them over fire. If you don't want to light the barbecue, the veggies can also be cooked on a gas stovetop or even in the oven.

SERVES 6

6 tomatoes
2 red capsicums (bell peppers)
1 green capsicum (bell pepper)
1 brown onion, unpeeled
3 long green chillies
6 garlic cloves, crushed
½ teaspoon ground cumin
80 ml (⅓ cup) extra virgin olive oil
sea salt flakes
challah, to serve

Prepare a charcoal barbecue and let the coals burn down to a coating of white ash.

Place the tomatoes, capsicums, onion and chillies over the charcoal and cook, turning often, for 30–40 minutes, until the skins are burnt and the insides are soft. The time this takes will depend on the strength of the heat. The tomatoes and chillies will cook more quickly than the onion and capsicums, so remove them when they are ready.

Once cooked, set aside to cool, then peel and discard the skins (you don't need to peel too perfectly as a bit of charred vegetable skin is good).

Chop the vegetables one by one into a chunky dip texture (this can also be done in a food processor using the pulse button). Transfer to a bowl and stir in the garlic, cumin and olive oil. Season with salt to taste.

Serve with fresh challah.

roasted eggplant, mango, amba, green chilli

This salad is inspired by the flavours of sabih, the legendary Iraqi-Jewish stuffed pita that is super popular at Very Good Falafel. When mangoes are in season we make it a lot, capitalising on the brilliant Iraqi idea to combine mango and eggplant.

SERVES 6

3 large eggplants (aubergines), cut into 2 cm (¾ in)
   thick rounds
sea salt flakes
extra virgin olive oil, for drizzling
1 mango, cut into 1 cm (½ in) cubes
¼ red onion, finely chopped
2 handfuls of coriander (cilantro), chopped
1 long green chilli, deseeded, finely chopped
1 teaspoon Amba (see page 180)

Preheat the oven to 180°C (350°F) fan-forced. Grease three or four large baking trays with olive oil.

Place the eggplant slices on the prepared trays, sprinkle with a little salt and drizzle with oil. Cook for 20 minutes, then turn the eggplant over, add a little more salt and oil and cook for another 20 minutes or until soft and golden. Allow to cool a little.

Combine the mango, onion, coriander, chilli and amba in a bowl. Season to taste with salt and about 1 tablespoon of olive oil. Top each eggplant slice with a little of the salad and serve.

peaches, basil, hazelnuts

Nothing could be more simple and summery than this salad! It's quick to make with just a few ingredients, but the peach juices, basil and hazelnuts together are just magic! A favourite at Very Good Falafel since the start, Shuki likes this salad with firm, less-ripe peaches but Louisa likes her peaches ripe and sweet.

SERVES 4

70 g (½ cup) hazelnuts
500 g (1 lb 2 oz) white or yellow peaches, as ripe
  as you like
bunch of basil, leaves picked
100 ml (3½ fl oz) extra virgin olive oil, or to taste
juice of 1 lemon, or to taste
sea salt flakes

Preheat the oven to 160°C (320°F) fan-forced.

Spread the hazelnuts over a baking tray and bake for 15 minutes or until fragrant and the skins begin to loosen. Allow to cool slightly, then rub the hazelnuts between your hands or in a clean tea towel to rub off most of the skins. Crush or roughly chop the hazelnuts.

Wash the peaches well, then remove the stones and slice each peach into wedges. Transfer to a large bowl, along with the hazelnuts. Add the basil leaves, plenty of olive oil, lemon juice and salt, to taste, then toss to combine and serve.

frozen grapes, herbs, zucchini flowers

Crunchy zucchini, bursting grapes, herbs and flowers.
Does life get any better?

SERVES 4

270 g (1½ cups) green seedless grapes
8 female zucchini (courgette) flowers, with baby
   zucchini attached
1 small zucchini (courgette), cut into ribbons
1 yellow (pattypan) squash, thinly sliced
½ red onion, finely chopped
small handful of coriander (cilantro) leaves
small handful of mint leaves
juice of ½ lemon
2½ tablespoons extra virgin olive oil, or to taste
sea salt flakes

Place the grapes in a zip-lock bag or airtight container, then set aside in the freezer for at least 3 hours or until frozen.

To prepare the zucchini flowers, slice the baby zucchini into rounds and pick and shred the flowers, discarding the stamens.

Place the zucchini flowers, grapes, zucchini, squash, red onion and herbs in a large bowl. Add the lemon juice, olive oil and salt to taste and toss gently to combine. Serve immediately.

cherries, walnuts, coriander, green chilli

We can see this bright, festive salad on the table in late December, when you might have lots of people over and various celebratory dishes to feast on.

SERVES 4 ·

50 g (½ cup) walnuts
500 g (1 lb 2 oz) cherries, pitted
½ red onion, finely diced
2 handfuls of coriander (cilantro), chopped
1 long green chilli, deseeded and finely chopped
juice of 1 lemon
80 ml (⅓ cup) extra virgin olive oil
sea salt flakes

Preheat the oven to 160°C (320°F).

Spread the walnuts over a baking tray and bake for 15 minutes or until fragrant and lightly coloured. Set aside to cool, then crush or roughly chop the walnuts.

Place the cherries, onion, coriander, chilli and walnuts in a large bowl. Add the lemon juice, olive oil and salt, to taste, and toss gently to combine. Serve immediately.

grilled apricot, warrigal greens, saffron oil, hazelnuts

Grilling apricots encourages them to release their natural sugars and gives them a deliciously charred flavour. If you are in Australia it is quite possible that warrigal greens are growing somewhere not too far from you, but if you can't put your hand on any, they can be replaced with spinach or leaf chicory.

SERVES 8

60 g (2 oz) hazelnuts
5 apricots, halved, stones removed
250 g (9 oz) warrigal greens, spinach or leaf chicory,
   leaves stripped
1 teaspoon sea salt flakes
juice of ½ lemon
Tahini sauce (page 11), to serve

SAFFRON OIL

250 ml (1 cup) extra virgin olive oil
pinch of saffron threads

Preheat the oven to 160°C (320°F) fan-forced. Preheat a barbecue grill to high.

To make the saffron oil, pour the oil into a small saucepan over very low heat and add the saffron. Infuse for about 15 minutes or until bubbles start to appear and the oil has turned orange. Set aside to cool.

Meanwhile, spread the hazelnuts over a baking tray and bake for 15 minutes or until fragrant and the skins begin to loosen. Allow to cool slightly, then rub the hazelnuts between your hands or in a clean tea towel to rub off most of the skins. Crush or roughly chop the hazelnuts.

Toss the apricot in a bowl with 2½ tablespoons of the saffron oil, then place on the barbecue grill and cook for 1–2 minutes each side, until charred.

Heat a large frying pan over medium–high heat and add the warrigal greens, pressing them down gently with a spatula until they start to wilt. Pour in 3 tablespoons of the remaining saffron oil, along with the salt, and toss to combine. Cook for 1–2 minutes until wilted, then add the lemon juice and remove from the heat.

Place the greens in a serving dish, top with the barbecued apricot halves and sprinkle with the hazelnuts. Serve with cold tahini.

Store leftover saffron oil in an airtight container in the pantry and use in dressings or the next time you fire up the grill.

chickpeas, fava, fresh tomato sauce

The smell of dried fava beans cooking is one of our absolute favourite things! In summer, served with ripe tomatoes, lots of olive oil and oregano, they are the dreamiest of legumes. We could eat this salad every day.

SERVES 8

1 cup (200 g) dried chickpeas (garbanzo beans), soaked
  in cold water overnight
1 cup (200 g) dried fava beans, soaked in cold water overnight
6 ripe tomatoes
1–2 garlic cloves, minced, to taste
120 ml (4 fl oz) extra virgin olive oil
sea salt flakes and freshly ground black pepper
juice of 1 lemon
½ red onion, finely diced
2 tablespoons shredded oregano leaves
2 tablespoons shredded mint leaves

Drain and rinse the chickpeas and fava beans. Add to separate saucepans of plentiful boiling water and simmer over medium heat for about 1 hour or until soft. Start checking at the 30-minute mark, as the time may vary depending on the age of the legumes and how long they have been soaking.

Next, score a shallow cross in the base of each tomato. Bring a saucepan of water to the boil, add the tomatoes and blanch for 2 minutes or until the skin starts to come away from the base of each tomato. Using a slotted spoon, scoop the tomatoes into a bowl of cold water and leave to cool. Peel the tomatoes, then roughly chop and place in a bowl. Stir in the garlic and 2 tablespoons of the olive oil, and season well with salt and pepper.

Drain the chickpeas and fava beans and place in a large bowl. Dress with the lemon juice, the remaining olive oil and salt, to taste, then add the onion and mix well. Top with the tomato sauce and herbs just before serving.

red capsicum involtini

Red capsicums are one of our absolute favourite vegetables. They are so versatile and with their brilliant red, they bring a lot of colour and flavour to the plate. Here, we roast them and cut them into strips to be filled with grains, capers and currants. Leave them to sit for an hour or two before you eat them, so the filling can soak up the capsicum juices.

MAKES 16

4 large red capsicums (bell peppers)
2 tablespoons extra virgin olive oil
2 garlic cloves, thinly sliced
shredded mint leaves and toasted pine nuts, to serve

CAPSICUM FILLING

100 g (½ cup) uncracked freekeh
50 g (⅓ cup) pine nuts
1 tablespoon currants, soaked in warm water
    for 10 minutes
1 tablespoon capers, rinsed and drained
2 tablespoons chopped mint leaves
50 g (1 cup) chopped parsley
finely grated zest and juice of 1 lemon
1 tablespoon extra virgin olive oil
sea salt flakes and freshly ground black pepper

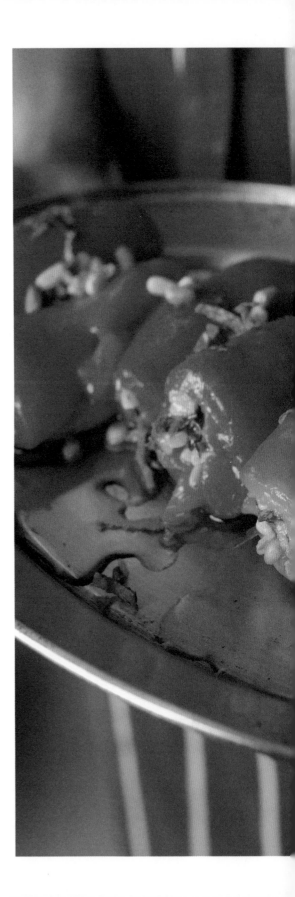

Preheat the oven to 200°C (400°F) fan-forced.

Put the capsicums on a baking tray and roast for about 35 minutes, until the skins are blackened and starting to separate from the flesh. Remove the capsicums from the oven, transfer to a bowl and cover until cool enough to handle. Carefully peel the capsicums and remove the seeds and stems. Split each capsicum into four long pieces.

Heat the olive oil a small frying pan over low heat. Add the garlic and cook, stirring, for about 2 minutes, until fragrant and golden. Remove the garlic with a slotted spoon and set aside on a plate. Reserve the garlic oil.

To make the filling, bring a saucepan of salted water to the boil over high heat. Reduce the heat to medium, add the freekeh and cook for about 30 minutes, until tender. Drain and spread on a tray to cool and dry.

Heat a frying pan over medium heat, add the pine nuts and toast, tossing frequently, for 2–3 minutes, until fragrant and golden.

Drain the currants, then combine with the freekeh, pine nuts and remaining filling ingredients in a large bowl and season, to taste. It should look slick with oil!

Spoon 1 tablespoon of the filling along each strip of capsicum, then roll up carefully and place on a serving plate. When you're done, top with the fried garlic, garlic oil, some shredded mint leaves and extra pine nuts.

tomatoes in pomegranate sauce

Tomato and pomegranate are probably the best-looking fellas in the market. Pomegranate, with its crown atop a slick leather jacket that keeps a million pink pearls safe; tomato and its soft shiny skin is just red best. Besides beauty, these two also share sweet and sour flavour elements, but of course each is very unique. Cooking the tomatoes in a pomegranate sauce is win-win – you get the best tomatoes and the best sauce as they do their give and take thing. The fried garlic and toasted hazelnuts ground the flavour and add that needed crunch.

MAKES 12

70 g (½ cup) hazelnuts
700 ml (23½ fl oz) pomegranate juice
1 teaspoon sea salt flakes
12 tomatoes (a few different varieties are best)
2½ tablespoons extra virgin olive oil
8 garlic cloves, thinly sliced

TIP

At the end of the meal, collect and chill any leftover sauce and use it as a salad dressing.

Preheat the oven to 160°C (320°F) fan-forced.

Spread the hazelnuts over a baking tray and bake for 15 minutes or until fragrant and the skins begin to loosen. Allow to cool slightly, then rub the hazelnuts between your hands or in a clean tea towel to rub off most of the skins. Bash the hazelnuts using a mortar and pestle, or in a food processor using the pulse function, making sure the nuts are still big enough to have bite.

Reduce the oven temperature to 150°C (300°F) fan-forced. Lightly grease a large flameproof casserole dish (Dutch oven) that will hold the tomatoes snugly.

Pour the pomegranate juice into a saucepan and add the salt. Bring to the boil over high heat, then boil for 2 minutes.

Place the tomatoes in the prepared dish and pour the pomegranate juice in between the tomatoes. Bake, covered, for 25 minutes, then remove the dish from the oven and place on the stovetop over medium heat. Gently simmer for 15 minutes or until the juice is reduced.

Increase the oven temperature to 180°C (350°F) fan-forced and return the tomatoes to the oven for a final 5 minutes, until golden. Allow to cool for a couple of minutes.

While the tomatoes are in the oven, heat the oil a small frying pan over low heat. Add the sliced garlic and cook, stirring, for 8–10 minutes, until the garlic is crispy. Remove with a slotted spoon.

Serve the tomatoes scattered with the garlic and hazelnuts and enjoy.

autumn

couscous from scratch —— chermoula baked vegetables —— pumpkin slices, spiced chickpeas —— roasted leek, pomegranate, walnuts, greens —— roasted quince, pearl barley, walnut, pistachio, saffron —— sweet potato and harissa gratin —— smoked grapes, pistachios, sumac, grains —— prickly pear, fresh za'atar, smoked almonds —— fennel, fresh borlotti, tomato —— stuffed silverbeet leaves in tomato–cinnamon sauce —— kohlrabi, citrus, olives, harissa oil —— grilled pumpkin, fried onion, date molasses —— stuffed figs

couscous from scratch

Growing up in Netanya, homemade couscous was all around me. My first girlfriend's family was from Algeria, one best friend was from Libya, another one from Morocco. It sometimes felt like every door I opened had a grandma shaking a sieve with fresh couscous falling through.

Ironically, the first time I came across a packet of instant couscous was in a cooking school in Australia. Our teacher told us that couscous was Italian and that there was no difference between the instant and the homemade version ... Oh how homesick I felt at the time.

FYI, the difference is like sleeping on rocks compared to sleeping on feathers.

It's a fluffiness you can't fake or beat.

For this recipe you will need a couscousier pan; all that means is a pan with a steamer attachment on top and a lid, a bit like a dumpling pan.

The recipe takes a bit of time but not much work at all, and of course a big smile awaits you at the end. Best served with a hot soup or stew on a cold day.

SERVES 6–8

1 kg (2 lb 3 oz) fine semolina
1 tablespoon sea salt flakes
250 ml (1 cup) olive oil

Tip the semolina and salt into a large bowl. Slowly, slowly, add 250 ml (1 cup) of water while rubbing and whisking the semolina with your hands. Once done, repeat with the oil until the semolina is well coated. Pass the mixture through a large flat fine-meshed sieve.

Half-fill the bottom part of a couscousier pan with water or soup and bring to the boil.

Place the semolina mixture in the top part of the pan and poke about six finger-sized holes into the mixture for the steam to go through. Cover with the lid and steam over medium heat for 45 minutes.

Place the couscous in a large bowl and spread it out. Slowly add 750 ml (3 cups) of water and mix using a fork (this might feel like a lot of water but it's crucial for a fluffy couscous), until the water is well distributed through the couscous.

Return the couscous to the couscousier and steam for another 20 minutes, then place the couscous back in the bowl and spread it out. Leave to cool to room temperature.

Working in a few batches, shake or push the couscous through the sieve into a bowl.

It's snowing couscous!

chermoula baked vegetables

This is a kind of vegetable pie, spicy and sweet with potatoes soaking up the chermoula. Perfect for autumn.

SERVES 6

bunch of silverbeet (Swiss chard)
8 desiree potatoes, thinly sliced
200 g (7 oz) butternut pumpkin (acorn squash),
    peeled and thinly sliced
sea salt flakes and freshly ground black pepper
extra virgin olive oil, for drizzling
½ red onion, sliced into rounds
½ × quantity Chermoula (see page 184)

Preheat the oven to 180°C (350°F) fan-forced. Grease a 25–27 cm (10–11 in) round baking dish with olive oil.

Remove the stalks from the silverbeet and tear the leaves into bite-sized pieces. Reserve the stalks for another use.

To assemble the bake, layer half the potato, slightly overlapping, over the base of the dish, then add all of the pumpkin, season with salt and pepper and drizzle with olive oil. Add the silverbeet leaves, then the onion and season again. Mix the chermoula with 125 ml (½ cup) of water and pour it over the top.

Layer the remaining potato on top and season with salt and more olive oil. Cover with foil and bake for 40 minutes. When the potato is very soft, remove the foil and cook until the potato is browned on top. Allow the bake to sit for 20 minutes before eating.

pumpkin slices, spiced chickpeas

We pretty much owe our lives to chickpeas. From the creamy hummus we sold during our early days at farmers' markets, to the crunchy falafels under the roof of the shop, and onwards to our current salad days. This recipe is an old favourite; first we boil the chickpeas until soft, then we fry them with a bunch of spices and rest them on a wedge of roasted pumpkin. Everybody who smells it wants a piece.

SERVES 6

1 cup (200 g) dried chickpeas (garbanzo beans),
    soaked in cold water overnight
½ butternut pumpkin (acorn squash), cut into
    2 cm (¾ in) thick slices
extra virgin olive oil, for drizzling
sea salt flakes
60 ml (¼ cup) vegetable or sunflower oil
5 garlic cloves, sliced
1 roasted red capsicum (bell pepper), cut into
    1 cm (½ in) pieces (see page 85)
1 tablespoon ground cumin
1 tablespoon sweet paprika
½ teaspoon smoked paprika
½ teaspoon freshly ground black pepper
½ lemon
coriander (cilantro) leaves, to garnish

Preheat the oven to 160°C (320°F) fan-forced.

Bring a large saucepan of water to the boil over high heat. Drain the chickpeas and add them to the pan, then reduce the heat to a simmer and cook for about 45 minutes, until tender. Drain.

Meanwhile, place the pumpkin in a roasting tin, drizzle with olive oil and sprinkle with a little salt, then transfer to the oven and roast for about 40 minutes or until the pumpkin is soft and caramelised.

Heat the vegetable or sunflower oil in a large frying pan over medium–high heat and fry the garlic for 2 minutes until golden. Reduce the heat to medium and add the capsicum, cumin, paprikas, 1 teaspoon of salt and the black pepper. Cook, stirring, for 30–60 seconds, until fragrant, then add the chickpeas. Toss together for 1–2 minutes, then remove from the heat and squeeze in the lemon juice.

Arrange the pumpkin on a plate, spoon over the chickpeas and garnish with coriander leaves.

roasted leek, pomegranate, walnuts, greens

The combination of pomegranate, roasted walnuts and greens always feels very festive to us.

Here we serve that goodness with leek that we first poach, then roast until golden.

SERVES 6

50 g (½ cup) walnuts
3 leeks
extra virgin olive oil, for drizzling
sea salt flakes
1 pomegranate, seeds removed
2 spring onions (scallions), sliced on the diagonal
small handful of dill fronds
small handful of torn mint leaves
juice of ½ lemon

Preheat the oven to 160°C (320°F) fan-forced. Lightly grease a baking dish.

Spread the walnuts over a baking tray and bake for 15 minutes or until fragrant and lightly coloured. Cool and chop the walnuts.

Trim the leeks by cutting off the dark-green ends, but keeping the root end attached.

Bring a wide deep frying pan of water to the boil over high heat, add the leeks, then reduce the heat to a simmer and poach for 10 minutes. Drain.

Once cool enough to handle, cut each leek in half lengthways, then shake in a bowl of cold water to get rid of any soil that might be hiding in the layers of leek.

Place the leek, cut-side up, in the prepared dish, drizzle with olive oil and sprinkle with salt, then transfer to the oven and roast for about 35 minutes, until tender and golden.

Meanwhile, mix the pomegranate seeds, spring onion, dill, mint and roasted walnuts in a bowl and season with salt and a little olive oil.

Transfer the leek to a serving dish and spread the pomegranate mixture on top. Squeeze over the lemon juice and serve.

roasted quince, pearl barley, walnut, pistachio, saffron

The combination of grains with the sweetness of fruit is one we really like. The fruit often appears in dried form, such as sultanas, but when quince are in season, this is our fruit of choice. We char the quince in a chargrill pan first, then glaze it with date molasses before roasting in the oven to get even more quince love.

SERVES 4

200 g (1 cup) pearl barley
pinch of saffron threads
40 g (⅓ cup) walnuts
40 g (1½ oz) shelled pistachios
3 quince
2 tablespoons date molasses
sea salt flakes
150 ml (5 fl oz) extra virgin olive oil, plus extra for drizzling
1 brown onion, sliced
wild fennel or fennel fronds, to serve
1 lemon, halved

Preheat the oven to 160°C (320°F) fan-forced. Lightly grease a roasting tin.

Bring a large saucepan of water to the boil over high heat. Add the barley, then reduce the heat to medium and cook for about 30 minutes, until soft. Drain and transfer to a large bowl. Immediately stir through the saffron.

Meanwhile, spread the walnuts and pistachios separately over a baking tray and cook for 8–12 minutes, until fragrant and lightly coloured. Leave to cool, then chop the nuts.

Cut each quince into quarters and scoop or cut out the seeds and the core.

Heat a chargrill pan over high heat until very hot, then add the quince and chargrill for about 2 minutes each side, until char lines appear.

Place the quince in the prepared tin, pour over the date molasses and sprinkle with a little salt. Transfer to the oven and bake for 8–10 minutes, until soft enough to bite.

Meanwhile, heat 2 tablespoons of the olive oil in a frying pan over medium heat and cook the onion for 15 minutes or until caramelised.

Add the caramelised onion, nuts, remaining oil and a few fennel fronds to the pearl barley. Squeeze in the juice of one of the lemon halves and season, to taste, with salt. Transfer to a serving dish and place the quince on top. Thinly slice the remaining lemon and add to the dish, along with a little more fennel.

sweet potato and harissa gratin

A thousand sweet potato suns, setting into an ocean of harissa with a garlic whirlpool … We love doing big bakes at the shop and this one always disappears very fast!

SERVES 6–8

1–1.2 kg (2 lb 4 oz–2 lb 10 oz) small sweet potatoes, peeled
80 ml (⅓ cup) Harissa (see page 176)
60 ml (¼ cup) extra virgin olive oil
sea salt flakes
1 garlic bulb, top cut off
1 tablespoon capers, rinsed (optional)

Cut the sweet potato into very thin slices, about 2 mm (⅛ in) thick, using a sharp knife or a mandoline. Transfer to a large bowl and add the harissa, olive oil and 1 tablespoon of salt. Use your hands to rub the ingredients into the sweet potato, then set aside to marinate for 1 hour.

Preheat the oven to 160°C (320°F) fan-forced. Lightly grease a 25 × 15 cm (10 × 6 in) baking dish.

Start layering the sweet potato slices vertically in the baking dish, then place the garlic bulb in the centre of the dish. Cover with foil, then transfer to the oven and bake for 1 hour. Remove the foil and cook the gratin for a further 15–20 minutes, until the top is lightly crisped. Scatter the capers over the top, if using, and sprinkle with a little salt.

Separate the soft garlic cloves and serve with the gratin.

smoked grapes, pistachios, sumac, grains

Smoking grapes over an open fire or barbecue is a wonderful way to cook this super-sweet fruit. You can also roast them in the oven if you don't have access to a fire.

SERVES 4

100 g (¾ cup) shelled pistachios
100 g (½ cup) cracked freekeh
1.5 kg (3 lb 5 oz) seedless red grapes, stems attached
handful of mint leaves, chopped
handful of parsley, chopped
½ red onion, finely diced
100 ml (3½ fl oz) extra virgin olive oil
juice of 1 lemon
sea salt flakes and freshly ground black pepper
1 teaspoon ground sumac

Preheat the oven to 160°C (320°F) fan-forced.

Spread the pistachios over a baking tray and cook for 8–10 minutes, until fragrant, taking care not to overcook. Leave the pistachios to cool, then finely chop.

Bring a saucepan of salted water to the boil over high heat, add the freekeh, then reduce the heat to medium and boil for about 15 minutes or until tender. Drain and spread the freekeh out on a tray to cool and dry.

Wash the grapes and place them over a fire to smoke. You can do this by suspending them with string about 75 cm (2 ft 4 in) above a campfire or placing them on a charcoal grill. Over the fire, they will take about an hour to smoke; on a grill it will be much quicker, about 15 minutes. Alternatively, increase the oven temperature to 180°C (350°F) fan-forced and roast the grapes on a baking tray for 20 minutes or until they are slightly shrivelled. Allow the grapes to cool, then remove the stems.

Mix the grapes, freekeh, herbs and onion in a large bowl. Dress with the olive oil and lemon juice and season to taste with salt and pepper. Transfer to a serving dish, sprinkle with the sumac and pistachios and serve.

prickly pear, fresh za'atar, smoked almonds

The first time I ate a prickly pear it was a prickly pear–flavoured icy pole.

They were very popular in Israeli summers during the 80s and definitely my favourite flavour. Sadly, big brands, such Nestle and Streets, entered the market in the 90s pushing out small producers, and with them the prickly pear icy pole became a nostalgic memory. I was only six years old.

Trying to save me from eating a tartrazine-soaked lemon icy pole instead, my uncle suggested we go get prickly pears ourselves, and it wasn't hard to find them.

Originating from the Americas, the prickly pear was brought to Spain and quickly spread all over the Mediterranean, becoming a much-loved fruit. It later arrived here in Australia, where it flourished so much it is now considered a weed in most states.

In order to get the fruit off the plant without being stabbed by the thorns, we use a metal tin with a sharpened edge, picking the fruit so the pear falls into the tin. Once in your kitchen, hold the pear with tongs and trim its edges with a sharp knife. Cut a line down through the skin, then peel it back while rolling the fruit out of its prickly jacket.

The flesh is sweet, juicy, healthy and definitely worth the effort. Oh and, yes, you eat the seeds too.

SERVES 4

5 prickly pears, peeled
¼ shallot, thinly sliced
small handful of smoked almonds, chopped
10 fresh za'atar or oregano leaves
1 tablespoon olive oil

Slice the prickly pear into 1 cm (½ in) thick slices and arrange on a plate.

Scatter the shallot, smoked almonds and herb leaves over the top. Drizzle with the olive oil and serve straight away.

fennel, fresh borlotti, tomato

*We love all pulses but fresh borlotti beans in particular
are an absolute treat. They taste nutty and their creamy
texture soaks up flavours beautifully. A nice simple way to
eat them in late summer and early autumn is to dress them
while warm with lemon, garlic, olive oil and lots of torn
basil. This recipe is a bit more hearty – the fresh beans
and chunks of fennel are baked in a tomato saffron sauce,
which turns them both golden and delicious.*

SERVES 4

300 g (10½ oz) fresh borlotti beans (or 200 g/1 cup dried
    borlotti beans soaked in cold water overnight)
sea salt flakes and freshly ground black pepper
1 bay leaf (preferably fresh)
2 tablespoons olive oil, plus extra to cook the beans
300 g (10½ oz) overripe roma tomatoes
1 fennel bulb
pinch of saffron threads (expensive and optional!)

If you're using fresh beans, pod them. If using dried beans, drain and rinse them well. From here, both go in a saucepan, covered by 5 cm (2 in) of water. Add a pinch of salt, the bay leaf and a good glug of olive oil. Bring to the boil, then reduce the heat to a simmer and cook for 10 minutes if using fresh beans and about 30 minutes if using dried. Remove the beans using a slotted spoon. Keep the bean cooking water!

Preheat the oven to 180°C (350°F) fan-forced.

Next, score a shallow cross in the base of each tomato. Bring the bean cooking water to the boil, add the tomatoes and boil for 2 minutes or until the skin starts to come away from the base. Using a slotted spoon, scoop the tomatoes into a bowl of cold water and leave to cool. Peel the tomatoes.

Remove the tough outer pieces of the fennel and cut the bulb into 1 cm (½ in) thick wedges. Reserve the fennel fronds. Heat the olive oil in a frying pan over medium heat and brown the fennel well for 3–4 minutes each side. Remove from the pan and season well with salt and pepper.

To the same pan, add the peeled tomatoes and cook with a little salt for about 10 minutes, until they start to break down.

Transfer the fennel and tomato to a small baking dish, add the saffron (if using), along with 125 ml (½ cup) of the bean cooking water to prevent the mixture from drying out. Transfer to the oven and cook for about 30 minutes until the fennel is very, very soft. Stir through the beans and cook for a further 10 minutes. Allow the mixture to sit for 10 minutes, then scatter the reserved fennel fronds over the top and start eating!

stuffed silverbeet leaves in tomato-cinnamon sauce

We use silverbeet leaves a lot at the shop: torn into stews and salads, blanched and dragged through garlic and chilli. This is a special way to cook the big, beautiful, slightly bitter leaves. We soften onion, celery and carrot into a sweet stuffing, then roll the stuffing in the leaves and poach them in a tomato and cinnamon sauce. As they cook, they become gentle and mellow! Break them open with a knife and fork and let the filling mix with the sauce.

SERVES 4

600 g (1 lb 5 oz) very ripe or tinned tomatoes
60 ml (¼ cup) extra virgin olive oil
1 garlic clove, smashed
1 cinnamon stick
2 brown onions, finely diced
2 celery stalks, finely diced
2 large carrots, finely diced
sea salt flakes and freshly ground black pepper
8 large silverbeet (Swiss chard) leaves, preferably intact,
    without holes

If you're using fresh tomatoes, score a shallow cross in the base of each tomato. Bring a saucepan of water to the boil, add the tomatoes and boil for 2 minutes or until the skin starts to come away from the base. Using a slotted spoon, scoop the tomatoes into a bowl of cold water and leave to cool. Peel the tomatoes and crush them with your hands into a bowl. Keep the cooking water.

Heat 2 tablespoons of the olive oil and the garlic in a large frying pan over low heat and cook for 1 minute or until the garlic is fragrant. Add the tomato and the cinnamon stick and simmer for about 20 minutes, until the oil floats to the top.

Meanwhile, heat the remaining olive oil in a frying pan over medium heat. Sauté the vegetables for 15 minutes or until they are softened, but not coloured. Season with plenty of salt and pepper and set aside to cool.

Remove the stalks from the silverbeet leaves, then shave the white end of each leaf.

Return the cooking water to the boil and blanch the silverbeet leaves, one at a time, for 2 minutes. Scoop out the leaves using a slotted spoon and plunge into iced water. When cool, place the leaves in front of you and add 1 tablespoon of the vegetable stuffing to the base of each leaf. Tuck in the sides and roll the leaves into eight parcels. Take a piece of plastic wrap and twist it around each parcel to make a ball shape. Unwrap the balls and transfer to the tomato sauce, then simmer for 30 minutes or until the sauce is reduced and thick.

Leave to sit for 20 minutes, or even a few hours before serving.

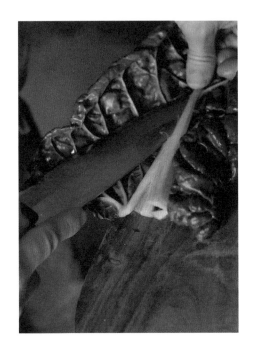

kohlrabi, citrus, olives, harissa oil

When we make harissa, we make sure we get every last little bit out of it. The oil that seals the harissa for storing is magical with many things, including this fresh, crunchy autumn salad of citrus and kohlrabi.

SERVES 4

1 grapefruit
1 blood orange
2 tablespoons harissa oil (see page 176)
juice of 1 lemon
extra virgin olive oil (if needed)
2 kohlrabi, peeled, cut into matchsticks
120 g (¾ cup) pitted green olives
handful of coriander (cilantro) leaves
sea salt flakes
sesame seeds, to serve

Remove the skin and pith from the grapefruit and orange, then use a small sharp knife to cut between the membranes and remove the segments.

Mix the harissa oil and lemon juice together. If you don't have enough harissa oil, make up the difference with olive oil.

Put the kohlrabi, citrus, olives and coriander in a bowl and pour the dressing over the top. Mix well, season to taste with salt, scatter with a few sesame seeds and serve straight away.

grilled pumpkin, fried onion, date molasses

Grilled pumpkin makes a nice change from roasted. It's less sweet and works really well here with fried onion and date molasses.

SERVES 4

1 kg/2 lb 3 oz butternut pumpkin (acorn squash), cut into 5 mm (¼ in) thick slices
2 tablespoons extra virgin olive oil, plus extra for drizzling
sea salt flakes
1 red onion, cut into 2 mm (¹⁄₁₆ in) thick slices
2 tablespoons red wine vinegar
2 tablespoons date molasses
1 tablespoon shredded mint leaves

Heat a large chargrill pan or barbecue grill to medium heat. When hot, add the pumpkin, drizzle with a little oil and cook for 8 minutes or until char lines appear on the base of each slice, then flip and cook the other side for a few minutes until the pumpkin is tender. Transfer to a serving plate, drizzle with olive oil and season with a little salt.

Heat the oil in a frying pan over medium heat, add the onion and cook, stirring frequently, for about 10 minutes, until softened. Add the vinegar, date molasses and a big pinch of salt. Let it bubble and reduce for 5 minutes.

Spoon the onion mixture over the pumpkin and finish with the mint.

stuffed figs

You've probably realised by now how much we like stuffing things ... we can't stop and it's the fig's turn this time. Figs are very easy to hollow out with a teaspoon, but don't remove too much because you still want that juicy fig flavour. Save whatever you do take out and if you didn't give it away already, just scatter it around the stuffed figs.

MAKES 12

2 tablespoons extra virgin olive oil, plus extra for drizzling
1 red onion, diced
1 garlic clove, crushed
1 tablespoon grape molasses
½ teaspoon baharat spice mix
200 g (1 cup) cracked freekeh, soaked in water for 1 hour
sea salt flakes and freshly ground black pepper
12 large figs
1 tablespoon chopped mint leaves

Preheat the oven to 180°C (350°F) fan-forced. Lightly grease a baking dish.

Heat the olive oil in a saucepan over medium heat. Add the onion and sauté for 10 minutes, until lightly golden. Add the garlic, grape molasses, baharat, freekeh and 125 ml (½ cup) of water. Cook, uncovered and stirring occasionally, for 10 minutes or until the freekeh is tender. Season to taste with salt and pepper.

Hollow out the figs by carefully cutting off the tops and using a teaspoon to scoop out a teaspoon's worth of fig flesh (keep the fig tops and flesh).

Stuff the figs with the freekeh mixture, then place their tops back on ad transfer to the prepared tray. Sprinkle with salt and pepper, drizzle with extra olive oil and bake for 10 minutes or until the figs are browned. Sprinkle the mint over the top and serve with any leftover freekeh and the reserved fig flesh scattered around the figs.

winter

whole cabbage stuffed with rice —— whole pumpkin —— mallow fritters —— kubba bi raz u patata —— carrot, green chilli, dates, orange —— lemon, mint, chilli flakes —— slow-cooked root vegetables with grains for a cold winter's day —— brussels sprouts, pilpelchuma, macadamias —— potato salad in radicchio leaves —— winter greens, fennel, citrus, green olives —— beetroot dip, pistachio hazelnut dukkah —— lupini beans, carrot, fennel, cumin —— white beans, brussels sprouts, capers —— potato, carrot, dried black olives, zhough

whole cabbage stuffed with rice

When it comes to cabbage we normally eat cold, hard cabbage. Other times, we divide and conquer, such as rolled cabbage leaves. But if you spend a long time with a cabbage – about 4 hours here – you get to meet its soft and sweet side. Give a cabbage the opportunity to be the star of the dinner table and it won't let you down.

SERVES 8

1 small plain white cabbage
400 g (2 cups) basmati rice, soaked in cold water for 10 minutes
sea salt flakes
160 ml (5½ fl oz) extra virgin olive oil
2 onions, diced
50 g (⅓ cup) pine nuts
1 teaspoon baharat spice mix
35 g (¼ cup) currants
freshly ground black pepper
½ bunch of dill, fronds finely chopped
½ bunch of mint, leaves finely chopped
½ bunch of parsley, finely chopped
250 ml (1 cup) vegetable stock

Preheat the oven to 180°C (350°F) fan-forced.

First you need to hollow out the cabbage. This might sound hard but it is actually pretty simple. Peel away the first few outer leaves and reserve them. Using a sharp knife, carve a 5 cm (2 in) deep square around the core of cabbage and gently tease it out.

Using a long-handled teaspoon and a small knife, start to shave and scrape out the inner leaves until you're left with three or four firm layers of cabbage. Reserve the scraped-out interior to make sauerkraut.

Drain and rinse the rice, then transfer to a large saucepan, cover with boiling water, season with salt and simmer over medium heat for 10 minutes. Drain and set aside.

Heat 60 ml (¼ cup) of the olive oil in a large frying pan over medium heat. Add the onion and cook for 5–10 minutes, until translucent, then add the pine nuts and baharat spice mix and cook for another minute. Add the currants, 1 teaspoon of black pepper and 2 teaspoons of salt and stir to combine. Remove the pan from the heat and stir the onion mixture and herbs through the rice.

Place the hollowed-out cabbage, hole side up, on a work surface and rub inside the hollow with 1 teaspoon of salt and about 1 tablespoon of the remaining olive oil. Stuff the rice mixture into the cabbage until it is full, but not firmly packed. Cover the hole with the reserved cabbage leaves, then turn the cabbage right side up and place in a roasting tin.

Pour the stock over the cabbage and into the roasting tin, along with the remaining olive oil. Season with a final teaspoon of salt and a little more pepper and cover the cabbage with foil. Transfer to the oven and roast for 1 hour, then reduce the temperature to 130°C (265°F) fan-forced and cook for another 30 minutes. Carefully remove the foil and continue to roast the cabbage for another 1 hour, 15 minutes, until golden brown and a bit burnt on top.

Slice once on the table. Bon Appetit!

whole pumpkin

This Armenian gift to the world is a real treat. The pumpkin has a big festive vibe and is normally served at weddings or Christmas parties, but no one will look at you weirdly if you bring it to a Halloween party either ... It's a great way to feed lots of people with one stellar dish and almost no dishes to wash.

SERVES 10

120 g (4 oz) walnuts
80 ml (⅓ cup) extra virgin olive oil, plus extra for drizzling
1 onion, diced
300 g (1½ cups) coarse bulgur wheat, soaked in hot water
    for 20 minutes
120 g (4 oz) organic dried apricots, sliced
30 g (½ cup) chopped dill
30 g (½ cup) mint leaves
1 teaspoon freshly ground black pepper
1 teaspoon ground cinnamon
1 teaspoon ground turmeric
1 cinnamon stick
3 teaspoons sea salt flakes
1 small Kent pumpkin (kabocha)
1 tablespoon grape molasses

Preheat the oven to 160°C (320°F) fan-forced.

Spread the walnuts over a baking tray and roast for 15 minutes or until fragrant and lightly coloured. Cool and break into small pieces.

Heat 2 tablespoons of the olive oil in a frying pan over medium heat. Add the onion and sauté for 10 minutes or until golden brown.

Drain the bulgur wheat and place in a bowl. Add the walnuts, onion, apricot, herbs, spices, 2 teaspoons of the salt and the remaining olive oil. Mix well.

Cut the top off the pumpkin, keeping the lid. Using a spoon, empty the seeds out and scrape the pumpkin smooth. Rub the grape molasses, remaining salt and a drizzle of olive oil into the interior of the pumpkin, then stuff it with the bulgur wheat mixture.

Place the lid back on, transfer to a baking tray and bake for 2 hours or until soft when pierced with a skewer.

Cut into wedges and serve.

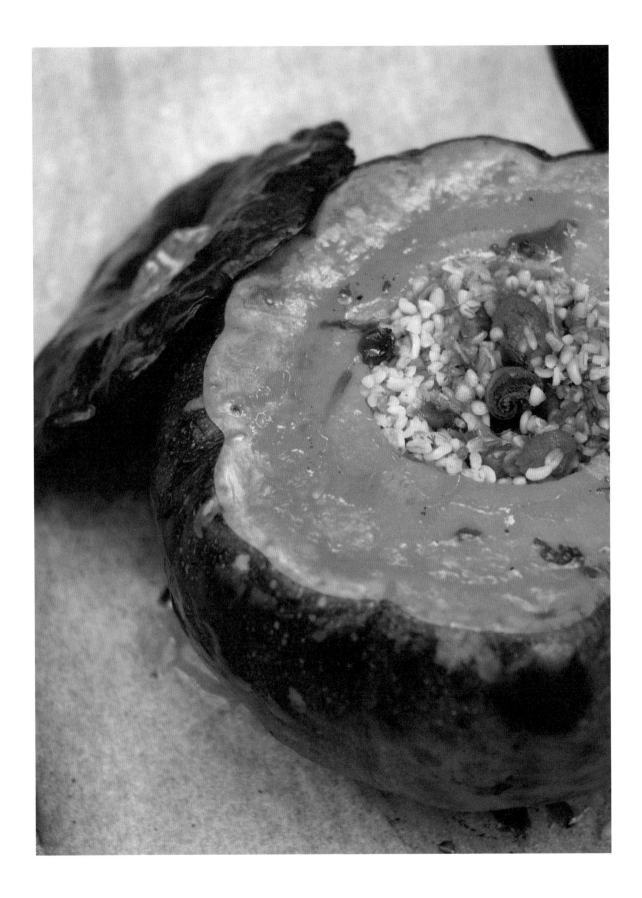

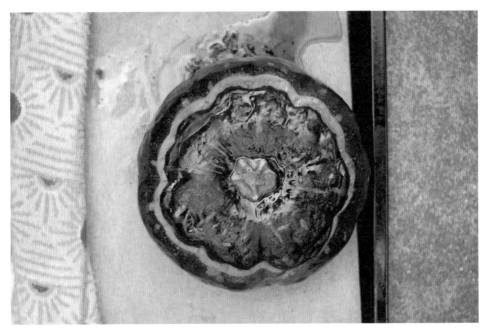

mallow fritters

Not many things beat the feeling of going for a walk in nature and coming home with a meal. Mallow is one of the most common weeds in the world – you can find it in parks, reserves, nature strips and even your own backyard. Easy to identify and pick, it is also nutritious. Here we use this simple ingredient to make delicious fritters.

MAKES 6

200 g (7 oz) mallow leaves
1 desiree potato, grated
75 g (½ cup) plain (all-purpose) flour
2 teaspoons sea salt flakes
1 teaspoon freshly ground black pepper
1 teaspoon ground turmeric
125 ml (½ cup) neutral-flavoured oil

TO SERVE

Amba (see page 180)
Tahini sauce (see page 11)
leafy salad

Blanch the mallow leaves in a saucepan of boiling water for 20 seconds, then drain and pat dry in a clean tea towel. Place the dried leaves in a large bowl and add the the remaining ingredients except the oil. Cover and set aside in the fridge for 30 minutes to firm up.

Drain and squeeze the mixture with your hands to remove any excess liquid, then form the mixture into six 6 cm (2½ in) round fritters.

Heat the oil in a large frying pan over medium heat. Cook the fritters for 3–5 minutes each side, until golden brown. Remove from the heat and drain on paper towel.

Serve with amba and tahini on the side, and a leafy salad.

kubba bi raz u patata

Nothing represents Jewish-Iraqi cuisine more than kubba (also known as kibbeh).

Kibbeh is easy to find all across the Levant in endless variations, the most common probably being Syrian fried kibbeh from Aleppo, with its shell of cracked bulgur wheat and a filling of lamb and pine nuts.

The version I grew up with, however, is very different. My mum would make the shell out of semolina, and instead of being fried the kibbeh (or kubba) would be poached in a soup like dumplings. The soup changed seasonally, with fresh garlic and mint in spring, sweet and sour tomato and okra in summer, pumpkin and sultanas in autumn and beetroot in winter. This was all well and good until Pesach (Passover) came along, and every year for one week we were not allowed to eat flour – including semolina and bulgur ...

Well, no one was gonna give up kubba for a week. The solution was kubba bi raz (rice kibbeh) or kubba patata (potato kibbeh) or a mixture of the two like the one here. This kubba is shaped like a torpedo and fried like the kibbeh from Aleppo. It's this mish-mash, thinking outside the box (or kubba shell) approach that enables us to enjoy kubba all year round!

MAKES ABOUT 20

100 g (2/3 cup) pine nuts
2 tablespoons extra virgin olive oil
1 onion, diced
350 g (12½ oz) button mushrooms, finely diced
3 garlic cloves, crushed
1 sprig of thyme
1 teaspoon baharat spice mix
sea salt flakes
½ bunch of parsley, chopped
400 g (2 cups) basmati rice, soaked in cold water for 1 hour
2 small potatoes, thinly sliced
1 teaspoon ground turmeric
freshly ground black pepper
vegetable oil, for deep-frying
Tahini sauce (see page 11), Amba (see page 180) and pickles,
    to serve

Preheat the oven to 160°C (320°F) fan-forced.

Heat a frying pan over medium heat, add the pine nuts and cook, tossing frequently, for 2–3 minutes, until fragrant and golden. Remove from the heat and set aside.

Heat the olive oil in a frying pan over medium heat. Add the onion and sauté for 10 minutes or until lightly golden, then add the mushroom, garlic, thyme and baharat spice mix. Season with salt and cook, stirring frequently, for 20 minutes. Remove from the heat and stir in the pine nuts and parsley.

Drain the rice and place in a large saucepan with the potato, turmeric and a good pinch of salt. Pour in enough water to cover the rice and potato by about 4 cm (1½ in), then bring to the boil over high heat. Reduce the heat to very low, cover with a lid and cook for about 30 minutes (adding a little more water if the rice starts to stick) or until the water evaporates and the rice is completely soft and broken down. Stir occasionally to avoid the rice sticking and burning on the base of the pan. Remove from the heat and stir through black pepper, to taste.

Using a potato masher, mash the rice and potato until combined and the mixture resembles a dough. Divide the dough into 20 balls somewhere between the size of a ping pong ball and a tennis ball. Using your fingers, flatten each ball into a circle in the palm of one hand, then stuff with a tablespoon of the mushroom mixture. Close the dough around the filling and roll it into a torpedo-like shape.

Heat the vegetable oil in a large saucepan or deep-fryer to 180°C (350°F) or until a small piece of kubba dropped into the oil sizzles. Working in batches, fry the kubba for 3–4 minutes, until crispy and golden. Remove from the oil using a slotted spoon and drain on paper towel.

Serve the kubba with tahini, amba and pickles on the side.

carrot, green chilli, dates, orange

We really like to take something standard like a boiled carrot and make it yummy. Carrots, dates and orange are a pretty unbeatable winter combination.

SERVES 4

8 carrots, cut on an angle into 2 cm (¾ in) pieces
sea salt flakes
100 ml (3½ fl oz) extra virgin olive oil
2 lemons
2 long green chillies, deseeded and finely chopped
6 Medjool dates, pitted and sliced lengthways into thin strips
1 handful of coriander (cilantro), finely chopped
finely grated zest of 1 orange

Put the carrot in a large saucepan, cover with water and add a pinch of salt. Bring to the boil, then reduce the heat to a simmer and cook the carrot for 10–15 minutes, until tender. Drain and cool slightly before dressing with the olive oil and juice of one lemon. Season with salt.

Remove the skin and pith from the remaining lemon, then use a small sharp knife to cut between the membranes and remove the segments.

Add the lemon segments, chilli, date and coriander to the carrot, mix well and taste for seasoning. Place on a serving plate and finish with the orange zest.

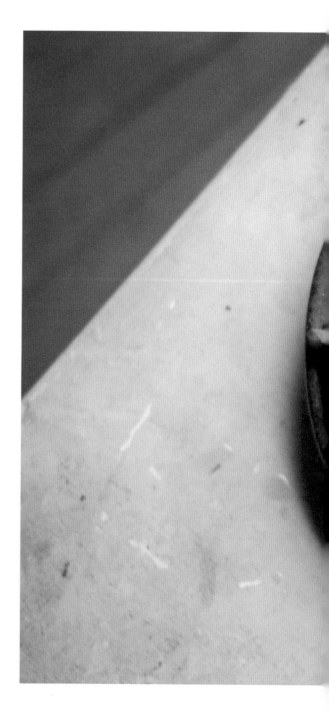

lemon, mint, chilli flakes

Probably the only salad in the book without lemon juice in its dressing :) Lemons in season are something to get out of bed for; their skin is just as valuable as their flesh and juice. This little side salad is the perfect accompaniment to a fried dish and, of course, would go so well with any other winter salads you put on the table.

SERVES 4

3 lemons with fresh, thin skin
8 mint leaves, shredded
2 tablespoons extra virgin olive oil
1 teaspoon sea salt flakes
1 teaspoon Urfa/Turkish black chilli (or regular chilli flakes)

Dice the lemons into 5 mm (¼ in) cubes, then transfer to a serving bowl.

Add the remaining ingredients and toss well to combine. Serve fresh.

slow-cooked root vegetables with grains for a cold winter's day

We recommend starting this recipe with a trip to your local farmers' market and grabbing as many different varieties of root vegetables as you can. All colours of carrot or beetroot, swede and turnip, parsnip and celeriac, onion and what not. They all look so fine under the rain and they will do the same in this dish. A new kind of Sunday roast.

SERVES 8

80 ml (⅓ cup) extra virgin olive oil, plus extra for drizzling

2 swedes, peeled and quartered

2 turnips, peeled and quartered

1 celeriac, peeled and quartered

8 small onions (pickling onions or shallots), peeled

1 garlic bulb, halved horizontally, plus 6 peeled cloves

600 g (3 cups) pearl barley, soaked in cold water for 3 hours

60 ml (¼ cup) date molasses

2 tablespoons Hawaij (see page 187)

1 tablespoon sea salt flakes

1 orange, halved or quartered

bunch of different-coloured baby beetroot (beets)

bunch of different-coloured Dutch carrots

1 parsnip, quartered lengthways

bunch of red grapes

bunch of oregano, plus extra leaves to serve

Preheat the oven to 130°C (265°F) fan-forced. Add a drizzle of olive oil to a large flameproof casserole dish (Dutch oven) or roasting tin.

Heat the olive oil in a large frying pan over medium heat and sear the swede, turnip and celeriac for about 5 minutes, until golden and crisp at the edges. Spoon into the prepared casserole dish or roasting tin. In the same frying pan, add the onions and garlic cloves and cook for 5 minutes, until lightly coloured.

Drain the barley and toss with the date molasses, hawaij, cooked onion and garlic and salt.

Spread the barley mixture over the top of the swede, turnip and celeriac and tuck in the halved garlic and orange pieces. Top with the beetroot, carrots with their leaves attached and the parsnip.

Pour 1 litre (4 cups) of warm water over the top, then bring to the boil. Reduce the heat to a simmer, cover with the lid or foil and leave to cook for 15 minutes.

Transfer the dish or tin to the oven and roast for 2 hours, checking every 45 minutes that the water hasn't reduced too much. If it's less than half the height of the dish or tin, add more water to reach this level, but don't add water in the last 30 minutes of cooking. Add the grapes and oregano in the last 10 minutes and remove the lid or foil.

Serve warm, with extra oregano leaves scattered over the top.

brussels sprouts, pilpelchuma, macadamias

Smoky pilpelchuma and sweet brussels sprouts make a legendary combination here! The macadamias are there for the crunch.

SERVES 4

200 g (7 oz) macadamia nuts
150 ml (5 fl oz) extra virgin olive oil
500 g (1 lb 2 oz) brussels sprouts, trimmed and halved
sea salt flakes and freshly ground black pepper
3–4 tablespoons Pilpelchuma (see page 187)

Preheat the oven to 160°C (320°F) fan-forced.

Spread the macadamias over a baking tray and cook for 8–10 minutes, until fragrant and lightly coloured. Leave to cool, then chop the macadamias.

Increase the oven temperature to 180°C (350°F) fan-forced. Heat 2½ tablespoons of the olive oil in a large frying pan over medium–high heat. Add the sprouts, cut-side down, and cook for 2 minutes, until golden brown.

Add the sprouts to a roasting tin and drizzle with 2½ tablespoons of the remaining olive oil. Season with salt and pepper, then transfer to the oven and roast for about 20 minutes, until soft. Remove from the oven, allow to cool a little and check for seasoning.

Spoon a little of the pilpelchuma onto the base of a serving plate. Pile the brussels sprouts on top and spoon over the remaining pilpelchuma. Finish with the macadamias and serve.

potato salad in radicchio leaves

I remember when we used to have family over for Shabbat lunch and I would ask Mum what she had prepared – she always said, 'I made this and that and mayonnaise'.

When she says mayonnaise she means a Russian-style potato salad with lots of dill, onion and … mayonnaise. It was never clear to me how this Russian dish became such a key part of this Iraqi woman's hosting repertoire, but it is delicious so it doesn't really matter anyway.

Lately, though, I started to see the downside of using so much mayonnaise and suggested to Mum that she use less. She didn't really like that and said she could use a mayonnaise 'diet' instead. Obviously not what I was after and maybe I shouldn't have said anything at all.

In this recipe we swap the mayonnaise with a preserved lemon paste; it has a similar texture to aioli and gives the salad a great twist.

SERVES 4

3 desiree potatoes, cut into 2 cm (¾ in) cubes
sea salt flakes and freshly ground black pepper
55 g (⅓ cup) shelled fresh peas
3 Preserved lemon quarters (see page 179)
2 spring onions (scallions), sliced
½ bunch of dill, fronds chopped
1 radicchio, leaves separated
2 tablespoons Harissa oil (see page 176)

PRESERVED LEMON PASTE

1 tablespoon liquid from the preserved lemon jar (see page 179)
80 ml (⅓ cup) extra virgin olive oil

Place the potato in a large saucepan and cover with water. Season with salt and bring to the boil over high heat, then reduce the heat to medium and simmer for about 10 minutes or until tender. Drain and transfer to a large bowl, then set aside to cool.

Blanch the peas in a saucepan of boiling water for 1 minute, then drain, refresh in cold water and add to the potato.

Separate the peel from the flesh of the preserved lemon, keeping the flesh for the paste. Slice the peel very thinly and add to the potato, along with the spring onion and dill.

To make the preserved lemon paste, place the preserved lemon flesh and a tablespoon of the liquid from the jar in a small food processor (or mortar and pestle). Process or grind the flesh to a purée, then, with the motor running, slowly drizzle in the oil. This will make an emulsion that looks like aioli but tastes better.

Add the preserved lemon paste to the salad and season with salt and pepper. Divide the potato salad among the radicchio leaves, drizzle with the harissa oil and serve.

winter greens, fennel, citrus, green olives

Salads like this one save the day in winter. Salty, sweet and citrusy, and crunchy enough to help you through the cold months. We make this all the time throughout winter when citrus and greens are in season.

SERVES 6

2 blood oranges
2 oranges
2 lemons
150 g (5½ oz) mixed winter leaves, such as leaf chicory,
    radicchio or kale, torn into bite-sized pieces
1 fennel bulb, thinly sliced, including fronds
½ red onion, thinly sliced
handful of green olives, pitted
100 ml (3½ fl oz) extra virgin olive oil
sea salt flakes and freshly ground black pepper

Remove the skin and pith from the oranges and one of the lemons, then use a small sharp knife to cut between the membranes and remove the segments. Place in a large bowl.

Add the winter leaves, fennel, onion and olives to the citrus segments. Mix the olive oil and juice of the remaining lemon together in a small bowl and season with salt and pepper. Pour over the salad and mix very well.

Serve immediately.

beetroot dip, pistachio hazelnut dukkah

This vibrant dip has been with us since our early farmers' market days. It's earthy, a bit sweet, creamy and crunchy, thanks to the dukkah. It makes a great snack with chopped veggies, salads or as is. For us, the only downside is when we get asked if it's a 'beetroot hummus'. No. There is no such thing as beetroot hummus.

SERVES 6

rock salt (optional)
2 beetroot (beets) (about 750 g/1 lb 11 oz)
250 ml (1 cup) extra virgin olive oil
280 g (1 cup) tahini
60 ml (¼ cup) date molasses
2 tablespoons ground cumin
2 tablespoons sea salt flakes
toasted bread, to serve

DUKKAH

35 g (¼ cup) hazelnuts
35 g (¼ cup) shelled pistachios
40 g (¼ cup) sesame seeds
40 g (¼ cup) nigella seeds
1 tablespoon cumin seeds
1 tablespoon coriander seeds
2 tablespoons sea salt

Preheat the oven to 160°C (320°F) fan-forced.

Pile the rock salt onto a baking tray and top with the whole beetroot. Roast for about 1½ hours or until soft when pierced with a skewer. Alternatively, wrap the beetroot in baking paper and roast for about 1½ hours, until easily pierced with a skewer.

Meanwhile, to make the dukkah, place the hazelnuts on a baking tray and toast in the oven for 7 minutes. Add the pistachios to the tray and toast for 8–10 minutes, until the nuts are toasted and golden. Remove from the oven, allow to cool a little, then rub the hazelnuts between your hands or a clean tea towel to remove the skins.

Heat a frying pan over medium–low heat, add the sesame and nigella seeds and toast, stirring frequently, for about 2 minutes. Add the cumin and coriander seeds and continue to toast, stirring, for 8–10 minutes, until fragrant.

Crush the nuts and seeds separately using a mortar and pestle, then combine in a bowl and stir through the salt. Set aside.

Peel the cooked beetroot and place in the fridge to cool. Once chilled, cut the beetroot into smaller pieces and place in a food processor. With the motor running, slowly add the oil, then transfer to a bowl. Add the remaining ingredients, except the bread, and stir until well combined.

Spoon the beetroot dip into a serving dish and sprinkle some of the dukkah on top. Serve with toast, if you like.

Store leftover dukkah in an airtight container or jar in the pantry for up to 2 months. It's really good on top of roasted veggies or an egg, if you're not vegan.

lupini beans, carrot, fennel, cumin

Lupini beans are very high in fibre and protein as well as zinc and magnesium. You will find the dried beans in spice shops and, although they require a couple of days of soaking, you handle them just like other legumes. In the Middle East, stalls selling lupini (known as turmus) with lots of cumin line the side of the road and it's a great snack for an evening stroll. Hence we couldn't separate the lupini and the cumin here either.

SERVES 5

400 g (14 oz) dried lupini beans soaked in cold water for
    48 hours (change the water after 24 hours)
1 onion, halved
5 carrots
3 lemons
50 g (⅓ cup) cumin seeds
sea salt flakes
2 fennel bulbs, cut into 8 wedges each
60 ml (¼ cup) extra virgin olive oil, plus extra for drizzling
bunch of coriander (cilantro) leaves

Drain the lupini and place in a large wide saucepan with the onion, one carrot, halved, one lemon, also halved, and 1 tablespoon of the cumin seeds. Cover with cold water and bring to the boil over high heat, then reduce the heat to medium–low and simmer for 2 hours, until the beans are soft but retain their bite, adding extra water if needed. Add 1 tablespoon of salt 10 minutes before removing the pan from the heat. Drain and discard the lemon, carrot and onion.

Preheat the oven to 160°C (320°F) fan-forced.

Cut the remaining carrots into 5 cm (2 in) long batons and spread over a baking tray, along with the fennel. Sprinkle with salt and drizzle with the olive oil. Roast for 15 minutes, then turn the vegetables over and roast for another 10 minutes or until golden and tender.

Toast the remaining cumin seeds in a large frying pan over low heat for 8–10 minutes, until fragrant. Crush the seeds using a mortar and pestle.

Remove the skin and pith from one of the remaining lemons, then use a small sharp knife to cut between the membranes and remove the segments.

Mix the beans, carrot, fennel and lemon segments in a large bowl. Squeeze in the juice of the remaining lemon, add the coriander leaves, crushed cumin seeds, a drizzle of olive oil and season with salt if necessary. Toss gently until combined and serve warm.

white beans, brussels sprouts, capers

We cook beans a lot at the shop! We always work with dried beans and dress them while warm, which allows them to beautifully soak up the flavours of the dressing and other ingredients. You can use a tin of beans though! The beauty of this salad is the contrast between the creamy beans and the crunchy sprouts and salty capers, and you can get that experience from tinned beans too. The sprouts are prepared three different ways here: raw, roasted and charred.

---

200 g (1 cup) dried cannellini or great northern beans, soaked in plenty of cold water overnight
100 ml (3½ fl oz) extra virgin olive oil
sea salt
1 bay leaf (preferably fresh)
juice of 2 lemons
200 g (7 oz) brussels sprouts, trimmed and halved
2 tablespoons salted capers, rinsed
large handful of parsley leaves

Drain and rinse the beans, then transfer to a heavy-based saucepan. Cover with cold water by at least 4 cm (1½ in) and add 1 tablespoon of the olive oil, a big pinch of salt and the bay leaf. Bring to the boil, then reduce the heat to a simmer and cook for about 1 hour or until tender (start checking after 30 minutes). The time it takes will depend on the age of the beans. Once the beans are tender, drain and place in a large bowl, season with salt, half the lemon juice and half the remaining olive oil.

Preheat the oven to 180°C (350°F) fan-forced. Lightly grease a baking tray.

Meanwhile, remove a single outer-layer leaf from each of the brussels sprouts and place on the prepared tray. Season with a little salt and roast for 5–10 minutes, until browned.

Thinly slice the rest of the sprouts. Heat a chargrill pan over medium–high heat and add one-quarter of the remaining sprouts. Cook, turning halfway through cooking, for 5 minutes each side, until char lines appear.

Toss the rest of the sprouts into a large bowl with the capers, parsley leaves, remaining lemon juice and remaining olive oil. Check for seasoning.

Put the beans on a platter and top with the dressed brussels sprouts. Finish with the charred sprouts and roasted leaves.

potato, carrot, dried black olives, zhough

We love to make salads like this one in winter – colourful and fresh but still warm and filling. The dried black olives are really great here but if you can't find any, just use regular black ones.

SERVES 4

4 carrots, cut on an angle into 2 cm (¾ in) chunks
4 desiree potatoes, scrubbed
sea salt flakes
handful of dried black olives, pitted
bunch of radishes, chopped into eighths
100 ml (3½ fl oz) extra virgin olive oil
juice of 1 lemon
2 tablespoons Zhough (see page 187)

Put the carrot and potatoes into separate saucepans and cover with cold water. Bring to the boil over high heat, then reduce the heat to medium, add a little salt and cook for 10–15 minutes, until tender. Drain.

When the potatoes are cool enough to handle, remove the skins and chop into similar-sized chunks as the carrot.

Place the carrot and potato in a serving bowl and add the olives and radish. In a separate small bowl, mix the olive oil, lemon juice and zhough until thoroughly combined. Season to taste with salt.

Pour the dressing over the vegetable mixture and gently combine. Let it sit for 10 minutes, then check for seasoning and serve.

shop things

falafel —— pita —— harissa —— preserved lemons —— amba —— fermented green mango —— torshi —— chermoula —— zough —— pilpelchuma

falafel

Here it is! The recipe that launched a shop, a market stall, the recipe that changed our lives!

The most important thing is freshness, so grind all of the ingredients right before rolling the falafel and frying in hot oil. Soak the chickpeas overnight in plenty of cold water, or for at least 12 hours, making sure they are covered by at least 10 cm (4 in) of water, otherwise they won't soak properly and your falafel will sadly fall apart. We use a mincer to grind the ingredients – they're inexpensive and will make a huge difference to your final falafel.

MAKES 25

500 g (1 lb 2 oz) dried chickpeas (garbanzo beans), soaked in cold water overnight or for at least 12 hours
2 onions, roughly chopped
5 garlic cloves, roughly chopped
bunch of parsley, roughly chopped
bunch of coriander (cilantro), roughly chopped
1 tablespoon fine sea salt
1 tablespoon ground coriander
½ teaspoon bicarbonate of soda (baking soda)
vegetable oil, for deep-frying

TO SERVE

Pita (see page 172)
Tahini sauce (see page 11)
chopped tomato and cucumber
pickles

Rinse the soaked chickpeas very well in cold water and drain well. Mix the chickpeas, onion, garlic and herbs together in a large bowl.

Fit a meat mincer with a 5 mm (¼ in) mincing plate. Pass the chickpea mixture through the grinder into a bowl, then repeat two more times.

Stir in the salt, ground coriander and bicarbonate of soda and mix very well to combine.

Heat enough vegetable oil for deep-frying in a deep-fryer or large heavy-based saucepan to 180°C (350°F), or until a small piece of falafel mix dropped into the oil sizzles.

Shape 1½ tablespoons of the falafel mixture into a golf ball–sized falafel, then repeat. Working in batches, fry the falafel for 3–4 minutes, until brown. Test one first to make sure the inside is cooked.

Remove from the oil with a slotted spoon and briefly drain on paper towel. Eat as soon as you can with pita, tahini, chopped tomato and cucumber and pickles!

pita

Fresh pita is one of life's great joys! Very Good Falafel would be nothing without the warm pita we get delivered every day. It's best eaten within a few hours of cooking, but leftovers are great fried and added to salads. You can rest the dough in the fridge overnight as well.

MAKES 16

500 g (3⅓ cups) plain (all-purpose) flour
1 teaspoon caster (superfine) sugar
2 teaspoons instant dried yeast
1 teaspoon fine sea salt
1 teaspoon baking powder

Stir the ingredients together in a large bowl. Pour in 300 ml (10 fl oz) of water and knead for 2–3 minutes, until you have a soft dough that's just slightly sticky.

Rest, covered with a tea towel, for 1–2 hours in a warm place. Divide the dough into 50 g (1¾ oz) pieces and roll into balls. You should get about 16. Using a rolling pin, roll into 15 cm (6 in) circles on a lightly floured surface.

Heat a heavy-based frying pan over very high heat. When the pan is as hot as you can get it, add one pita at a time and cook for about 3 minutes – it should puff up – then flip over and cook the other side for 3 more minutes, until cooked through with a little colour.

Pile up the cooked pita, covered with a tea towel, while you work on the rest. Serve within a couple of hours of making.

harissa

Let's pause for a second and acknowledge that we are here to talk about the greatest condiment of all time: harissa. This is definitely what we would take with us to a deserted island.

In the shop we add harissa to all kinds of salads. It is great with potatoes, sweet potatoes and pumpkin, and also with raw veggies, such as carrot, kohlrabi or fennel, and even with citrus!

We love making it with a fair bit of oil, so then we also have the tastiest oil to use for dressings.

In the motherland of harissa – Tunisia – it is made with dried baklouti peppers which are long, red and not so spicy. If you can't put your hand on them, Mexican guajillo or Macedonian ajvar make good replacements. Whatever you use, just make sure the peppers are long and mild and NOT small and spicy.

We break with tradition a bit by adding preserved lemons to ours; you gotta trust us, it don't do no harm.

MAKES 400 ML (13½ FL OZ)

200 g (7 oz) dried baklouti peppers
5 garlic cloves
1 whole Preserved lemon (see page 179)
1 teaspoon sea salt flakes
½ teaspoon crushed caraway seeds (optional)
180 ml (¾ cup) extra virgin olive oil, plus extra to cover

Place the peppers in a large bowl and cover with warm water. Soak for 30 minutes or until softened. Drain.

Split the peppers and discard the seeds and stalks. Using a mincer, grind the soaked peppers, garlic, preserved lemon, salt and caraway seeds (if using) into a bowl. Lastly pour the oil slowly through the mincer; it will collect all the flavours that were left behind. Mix well.

Alternatively, blend all the ingredients in a food processor until finely chopped, then pour in the oil until incorporated.

Spoon the harissa into a clean jar, cover with a good layer of olive oil and store in the fridge for up to 3 months.

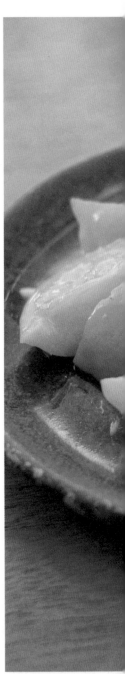

We love it when life gives us lemons. We preserve them!

Preserved lemons are a key ingredient in our salads at the shop. We also add them to potatoes, artichokes, sauces, salsas and what not. We also don't waste a drop of the liquid they're preserved in or their flesh – it is all gold!

Most recipes preserve the lemons in a mixture of salt, lemon juice and water but we omit the water, which makes the liquid in the jar turn almost jelly-like. We later blend this with the lemon flesh and turn it into a paste by slowly adding olive oil (see page 151).

FILLS 1 × 1 LITRE (34 FL OZ) JAR

4 lemons
140 g (½ cup) fine sea salt
1 small dried chilli
5 coriander seeds
freshly squeezed lemon juice, to fill the jar

Cut three of the lemons into four wedges each. Dip each wedge in the salt on both fleshy sides, then transfer to a clean 1 litre (34 fl oz) jar, seal with the lid and set aside in the pantry for 3–4 days.

After 3–4 days the lemons will have juiced out their liquid and the jar should be about half-full of lemon juice. You should also have space for the remaining lemon (or at least half) to go in now – dip it in salt and add to the jar. Add the dried chilli and coriander seeds, then fill the jar to the top with freshly squeezed lemon juice. Seal with the lid and set aside in a shady area for 2–3 weeks or until the skin is soft and the bitterness has disappeared.

Once ready, keep the jar in the fridge where the preserved lemons will keep for up to 1 year.

amba

The story of Iraqi Jews begins between 597–586 BC and an event known as Babylonian captivity. The strategy of king Nebuchadnezzar II was to expel some of the population of his conquered cities in order to destabilise them and put these skilled captives to work back in Babylon.

In 539 BC the Persian empire conquered Babylon and allowed the Jews to return to Judea, however many of them decided to stay in Babylon, turning it into a thriving centre for Jewish learning.

Fast forward to the 17th and 18th centuries when Iraq was under Ottoman rule and the sultan had made things a lot harder for the Jewish community. Many of them, especially traders, decided to flee to India until better times returned. There, they were exposed to mango chutney and they were blown away. They quickly learned the art of making this condiment, and with their own tweaks and adjustments they created amba.

Coming back to Iraq years later, amba was welcomed with open arms. These days, no Iraqi can imagine eating falafel or shawarma without it.

At our shop it is very easy to identify our Iraqi customers as they always ask for extra, extra, extra amba. We totally understand. It is Iraqi umami and we absolutely love it!

MAKES 330 ML (11 FL OZ)

3 teaspoons ground fenugreek
2 teaspoons ground turmeric
1 teaspoon mustard powder
1 teaspoon hot paprika
1 teaspoon sweet paprika
1 teaspoon citric acid
160 g (½ cup) Fermented green mango (see page 183)
250 ml (1 cup) fermented green mango liquid (see page 183)
juice of ½ lemon

Combine the spices and citric acid in a bowl, then add the fermented green mango, along with the liquid. Stir through the lemon juice and mix well. The amba should be a creamy consistency. If it's too thick, add a little water.

Store in a clean 330 ml (11 fl oz) jar in the fridge for up to 6 months. Serve the golden liquid with falafel, sabih, shawarma or as part of a mezze spread.

fermented green mango

MAKES 1 KG (2 LB 3 OZ)

1 kg (2 lb 3 oz) green mangoes, peeled and seed removed, flesh
    cut into 1 cm (½ in) pieces
3 tablespoons fine sea salt

Fill a 1 litre (34 fl oz) jar three-quarters full with the mango.

Stir 1 tablespoon of the salt into 250 ml (1 cup) of water
until dissolved. Add another tablespoon of salt and
another cup of water and stir until dissolved, then repeat
with the final tablespoon of salt and a final cup of water.
Pour the brine over the mango in the jar, leaving a 1 cm
(½ in) gap at the top. You may not need all of the liquid.

Close the lid and place on a kitchen bench away from
direct sunlight. For the first 4 days, open the lid each day
to let some gas out, then leave in the pantry for a further
10 days, unopened.

After 2 weeks the mango is ready and needs to be placed
in the fridge. It will keep for up to 1 year.

torshi

In a shaded corner of our kitchen you can always find a big jar of torshi. Originating from the Persian word 'torsh', which means 'sour', these Iraqi/Iranian pickles are the perfect companion for falafel, but also just the best meal between meals you can have. There are a million different combinations of ingredients and techniques to make torshi, but this is our favourite.

Make sure you use fresh, crunchy veggies in order to receive juicy, crunchy pickles.

MAKES ABOUT 1 KG (2 LB 3 OZ)

½ red capsicum (bell pepper), cut into 3 cm (1¼ in) pieces
½ green capsicum (bell pepper), cut into 3 cm (1¼ in) pieces
1 carrot, cut into 1 cm (½ in) thick slices
200 g (7 oz) white cabbage, cut into 2 cm (¾ in) pieces
¼ small cauliflower, separated into florets
125 ml (½ cup) white vinegar
1 garlic clove
1 Thai green or bird's eye chilli
1 teaspoon ground turmeric
1½ tablespoons fine sea salt
1 tablespoon Amba (see page 180)

Mix the veggies together and place in a clean 1 litre (34 fl oz) jar. Add the remaining ingredients, then fill the jar with water, leaving a 1 cm (½ in) gap at the top. Seal the jar and shake well.

Leave the jar on a kitchen bench away from direct sunlight for 4 days, shaking the jar every day.

Eat straight away or keep in the fridge for up to 2 months.

chermoula

Born in Morocco, chermoula is a mix of herbs, garlic, spices and sometimes chilli. We like it with roasted root vegetables to bring freshness and warmth through the colder months. Our version has lemon for extra sunshine.

MAKES 375 ML (1½ CUPS)

2 garlic cloves
1 lemon, skin, pith and seeds removed, flesh chopped
2 tablespoons extra virgin olive oil
bunch of parsley, roughly chopped
bunch of coriander (cilantro), roughly chopped
1 tablespoon ground turmeric
1 tablespoon smoked paprika
1 tablespoon ground cumin
1 tablespoon sea salt flakes

In a food processor, preferably, or with a stick blender, blend the garlic and lemon to a smooth paste, adding a little of the oil to get things going a bit. Add half the herbs and blend until smooth, then add the rest of the herbs and blend again. When you have a fine paste, scoop the mixture into a bowl and add the spices and salt. Fold through the remaining olive oil and check for seasoning.

Store the chermoula in a jar in the fridge for up to 4 days.

zhough

Zough is a Yemenite sauce made with chillies, herbs and spices. This recipe comes from my friend's dad Moti, who is from Sana'a in Yemen.

MAKES 625 ML (2½ CUPS)

2 bunches of coriander (cilantro) leaves
350 g (12½ oz) long green chillies, chopped
15 garlic cloves, chopped
12 small dried red chillies, roughly chopped
1 teaspoon ground cumin
½ teaspoon ground cloves
1 teaspoon hawaij (see below)
½ teaspoon sea salt flakes
½ teaspoon ground cardamom
80 ml (⅓ cup) olive oil

HAWAIJ

3 tablespoons freshly ground black pepper
3 tablespoons ground cumin
1 tablespoon ground coriander
2 teaspoons ground turmeric
1 teaspoon ground cardamom

For the hawaij, mix the ingredients together and store in a jar for up to 6 months.

Process the coriander leaves and green chilli in a food processor until finely chopped. Add the garlic, dried chilli, cumin, cloves, hawaij, salt and cardamom and process until smooth. Transfer to a bowl and stir in 2 tablespoons of the olive oil until combined.

Place the zough in an airtight container and cover with the remaining olive oil.

Seal and refrigerate for up to 1 month or freeze for up to 2 months.

pilpelchuma

'Pilpel' means 'peppers' and 'chuma' means 'garlic'. This paste, which originates from Libyan Jews, is so quick to make and lifts any dish it touches. My mum calls it 'the working mum's harissa' because, although it's a lot like the spicy paste, it's a lot less messy to make, you usually have all the ingredients on hand and it takes less than 5 minutes to put together.

As a kid, my parents used to spread it on a piece of challa to shut me up until the kubba (see page 138) was ready. I did shut up, but then asked for more.

Use pilpelchuma as a spread or a paste, as a salad dressing or in your shakshuka to make it taste right. Once you start including it in your cooking, you won't be able to stop.

MAKES ABOUT 250 ML (1 CUP)

1½ tablespoons smoked paprika
1 tablespoon sweet paprika
1 tablespoon hot paprika
1 tablespoon ground caraway
2 teaspoons ground cumin
4 garlic cloves, crushed
1 tablespoon sea salt flakes
250 ml (1 cup) extra virgin olive oil
juice of 1 lemon

Place the spices, garlic and salt in a bowl, then add the oil while stirring constantly. Add the lemon juice and stir to combine.

Store in a jar in the fridge for up to 6 months.

thanks

This book is dedicated to our parents, Shlomo and Tikva, Graham and Jeannie. Thank you for believing in us and teaching us to love our vegetables!

We want to give thanks to the following people for helping us bring this book together!

To Madz, for your amazing photos, support and organisation.

To Rosa, for your patience and enthusiasm, even though you never ate any of the food.

To Garlic, for always being there.

To our families, George, James, Mary Jane, Jack, Ramya, Alexandra, Ingrid, Ari, Lior, Amit, Roni, Ailsa, Dalia, Meir, Herzel, Dov.

To Gabriel, for scaling the fish, trying the food and looking after the child.

To all the staff at Very Good Falafel for everything you do every day.

To the customers that let us make them falafel, which makes our dreams come true.

To Cultivating Community for lending us the kitchen that let us start our business.

To Melbourne Farmers Markets, for your support and encouragement eight years ago!

To all our suppliers, for the best vegetables, tahini and olive oil.

To Sam and his trolley from Brunswick Market, for always bringing the vegetables.

And lastly, to each other! We have been in business together for eight years and every day we are thankful to have a friend to share the load, who loves the same food and the same jokes.

about the authors

Hailing from the seaside town of Netanya in Israel, Shuki Rosenboim's world of food has been guided by his mother's obsession with feeding others and his father's love of healthy produce. Enthusiastic in his work, Shuki loves to make people happy through cooking, especially when the ingredients are harvested from his Coburg garden.

After moving to Australia 15 years ago, Shuki started work as a kitchen-hand at Chapel Street's Caffe e Cucina, which sparked an addiction to the energy of commercial kitchens. In between playing soccer and singing in local punk band The Shabbab, Shuki's food career has flourished, culminating in Very Good Falafel. Melbourne's north is now his home.

Louisa Allan was born in the Mallee town of Wycheproof and spent her childhood on a grain and pulse farm, where she loved to cook and experiment with recipes for friends and family. After several years as a primary-school teacher, Louisa became a full-time hummus and falafel maker with Shuki. She lives with her daughter in Brunswick, Melbourne, and loves to feed falafel to the community.

Shuki and Louisa acknowledge that the Wurundjeri clan are the custodians of the land on which this book was made, and we pay our respects to Elders, past, present and future.

index

Published in 2022 by Smith Street Books
Naarm | Melbourne | Australia
smithstreetbooks.com

ISBN: 978-1-9224-1786-2

CIP data is available from the National Library of Australia

Publisher: Paul McNally
Senior editor: Lucy Heaver, Tusk Studio
Designer: Vanessa Masci
Cover designer: Vanessa Masci
Photographer: Madz Rehorek
Typesetter: Megan Ellis
Proofreader: Rachel Carter
Indexer: Helena Holmgren

Printed & bound in China by C&C Offset Printing Co., Ltd.

Book 224

10 9 8 7 6 5 4 3 2 1